Cricket is for Fun

Harry East

A Second Innings from
Yorkshire's Golden Age

The Whitethorn Press Limited

By the same author:
Laughter at the Wicket

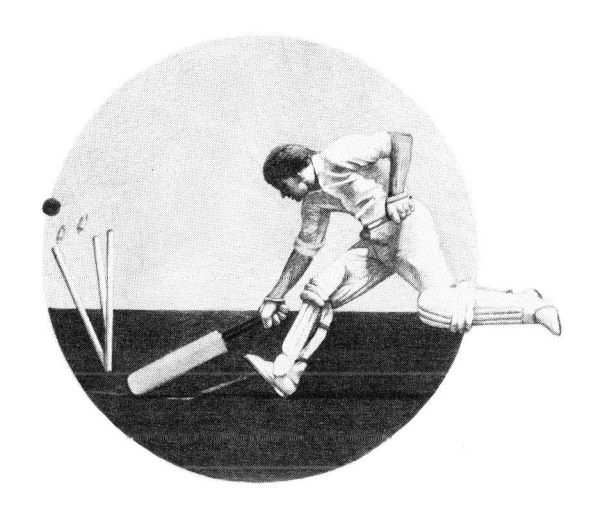

Dedicated...
To Stephen, who sympathises with Kipling.

Published by
The Whitethorn Press Limited
Thomson House, Withy Grove
Manchester M60 4BL

Litho Preparation and phototypeset by
Lapex Graphics Limited, Heswall

Printed in England by
E. J. Arnold & Son Ltd.

© Harry East 1981

No part of this publication may be reproduced, stored in a retrieval system or transmitted in any form or by any means, electronic, mechanical, recording or otherwise, without the prior permission of the publishers.

ISBN 0 9506055 8 1

Contents

Prologue **7**
Captains **9**
More Captains **18**
Captain, my Captain **23**
Tales from the Ale Tent **25**
Heroines of the Tea Tent **29**
They also Serve **35**
Umpires **39**
More Umpires **42**
Marriage Guidance **46**
The Knight that Might Have Been **50**
Sackcloth **53**
. . . and Ashes **58**
Shipmates Ashore **62**
'Ten Ale Cans' **69**
Swansongs **73**
Epilogue **80**

Acknowledgements

My sincere thanks are due, in general, to all those dedicated men and women who toil, unsung and unrewarded, throughout the year that village cricket may survive; in particular to the players, officials, members and tea tent ladies (though my wife would list them in the reverse order) of Buttershaw St. Paul's Cricket Club, who make the Saturday afternoons of our geriatricity so pleasant: to the editors of *Yorkshire Life* and the *Yorkshire Ridings Magazine* for permission to use material already published, and, on a personal note, once more to Maurice Colbeck, whose sympathy, expertise, kindness and advice have made this book possible.

HARRY EAST

In addition to those named above, the publishers wish to thank the following for permission to reproduce photographs, etc. Miss Mollie Staines, p32; Central Press and Telegraph and Argus for D. R. Jardine, p63; MCC for the Hon. F. S. Jackson, p9 and cover; Warwick Armstrong, p10; Lord Tennyson, p11; 'Tossing up', p13 and cover; Lord Hawke, p18 and cover; Ted Wainwright, p37; Wilfred Rhodes, p54; Bobby Peel, p56; George Ulyett, p68 and cover; Tom Emmett and Billy Bates, p69; M. W. Booth, p76; Yorkshire Post for F.E. Greenwood and A. B. Sellers, p20; George Hirst, p53; George Macaulay, p59; George Freeman, p73; Wilfred Rhodes, p74; Hedley Verity, George Hirst, p78. We apologise for any unwitting omissions or infringements and will be glad to correct them in future editions.

Pencil drawings by Edward Bates
Cartoons by Ernest Andrew

PROLOGUE

When the County Cricket Championship is in full swing there are 187 first-class cricketers playing. They are cocooned by their acolytes and myrmidons, their coaches, managers, promoters, press agents, ghost writers and statistical analysts. And none of them is of the slightest importance.

Cricket was neither born nor succoured on the mighty Test Match grounds of Lord's, the Oval, Trent Bridge or Old Trafford with their opulent pavilions, their printed score cards, their members' enclosures, their club ties, their computeresque score boards, their indoor schools, their immolation of all things jolly, earthy and natural to the stultifying exactitude of a science.

But it is there cricket will die unless the common man, made in God's own image, not spawned by political science or economic theory, asserts himself and annihilates the hydra-headed dragon of sponsorship, flood-lit abomination, yellow pads, crimson umpires' coats, Sunday afternoon's tawdry caricature and the tarnishing of a noble game to the whims of those who will defile its purity for greed and gold.

For cricket was bred on the village greens of old England, nestling, actually and metaphorically, in the shadow of pub and parish church.

It is probable that no atheist was ever a good cricketer. Indeed, in the days when God still held sway over Mammon, wise Church Councils were aware that their incumbent's prowess on the cricket field on Saturday was as important as his performance in the pulpit on Sunday.

One West Riding Church Council, their leader having departed to greener pastures, invited a possible successor to spend a weekend in the parish. He arrived on a Friday evening, and having been made welcome and comfortable, was asked, 'Has tha brought thi cricket flannels?'

The candidate wondered if he'd heard aright.

'Tha sees', explained his interrogator, 'tha'rt expected to laik for t'Sunday school team tomorn. But don't fret thisen. We can borrow thi some.'

So he travelled to the away game, and after the match, along with his team mates, crossed to the 'Woolpack' to recharge his batteries. On Sunday, he stumbled somehow, through two services.

On the following evening, when the Church Council assembled in full panoply, opinions and ideas on various topics were tossed to and fro until, eventually, all eyes were turned to the senior elder.

'Well', mused that worthy, 'Ah must say he seems more comfortable at t'back of a pint than in t'front of a pulpit. When I quoted to him, "The mountains shall be molten under him, and the valleys shall be cleft as wax before the fire", he said it were from Malachi, and if he'd studied his Bible, he'd hev *known* it were from Micah. He nobbut prayed for twenty-five minutes, and he didn't pick *Onward Christian Soldiers* for t'first hymn, even though we'd won on t'Saturday! But he's a lovely square cut. Ah think we'll set him on . . .'

George Borrow, in his *Wild Wales*, said he could recognise Methodism by 'oats and poverty', but before the World Temporal usurped the World Spiritual, the glory of the Sunday services was preceded by the joy of the Saturday afternoon's cricket match. Due to Methodism's past rancours the sect developed almost as many facets as God's House has mansions. But, on Saturday afternoons, the Wesleyans, the Primitive Methodists, the New Wesleyans, the United Methodists, the Reformed Methodists besported themselves and joined in conflict with the Baptists, the Anglicans, the Congregationalists, the Unitarians and the Good Templars so that two league points might be won and, on their Sportsman's Sunday, praises both to God and the cricket team could ring through the chapel.

The salvation of cricket lies on the village greens and in the chapels of England. No man, certainly no cricketer, can serve two masters, and as long as Mammon flourishes with his bag of gold, prostituting the game as a gimmick for the advertising boys, cricket will wither.

When the Angel writes in his Book of Gold there will be other names along with Abou Ben Adam's . . . the names of the down-trodden who rolled the wicket, whitened the pads, washed the umpires' jackets, swept out the dressing tent, ran raffles and pie suppers in winter to raise funds, mended the seats that the vandals had damaged, glazed the cottage windows broken by lofted cow shots, put up the nets on practice nights and paid the umpires out of their own pockets when the kitty had run dry.

In vain shall we look for those whose deeds filled the morning papers, who travelled to the four corners of the earth to ply their lucrative craft.

The camel struggling through the eye of the needle had an effortless task compared with that of the glamour boys beating despairingly on the locked covers of Leigh Hunt's Golden Book.

CAPTAINS

Many tomes have been written on the art of captaincy. Philosophers have delved into the psychology required for the post and into the modern sciences of man-management and industrial relations. They have advised on the study of ground and weather conditions and on the wisdom of discussing wear and tear of the pitch with the groundsman. Advice from the team selection committee, they suggest, should be encouraged and assimilated; the strengths and weaknesses of the opposition analysed.

In the past this was done with that most valuable adjunct to every cricket team, the bag-carrier. But he, alas, has disappeared, thrown to the dogs in this age of petrol engines, just as the bag is thrown into the boot of a car.

He has been replaced by an individual with the ostentatious title of physiotherapist. Medical science has discovered tendons, ligaments, hamstrings and discs, and, before play starts, a morning surgery has to be held to assess the

'The greatest captain of all time . . . the Hon. Stanley Jackson.'

Warwick Armstrong, 'the Australian behemoth'.

aches and pains, physical trials and tribulations of the squad.

There was no such nonsense fifty years ago. Yorkshire, except when most of the team were required for a Test Match, played the same eleven throughout the season. There were no masseurs, medical orderlies or psychiatrists engaged as camp followers or fellow travellers.

Expressing concern at this modern trend, I once asked Emmott Robinson, veteran Yorkshire all-rounder, 'Did you never have any injuries, Emmott?'

'When Ah did t'hat trick against Sussex in 1928', he told me, 'Ah'd two broken ribs'. Noting my surprise, he added, 'Tha sees, in them days, if we didn't laik, we didn't get paid.'

Any theoretical analysis of captaincy requirements is, of course, a load of rubbish. A good captain is the leader of a team that wins its matches – by fair means, if possible, but by foul means rather than suffer defeat.

The greatest captain of all time was of course a Yorkshireman, the Honourable Stanley Jackson, who captained England against Australia in 1905. He won the Test Matches by two to nil with three drawn; he won the toss in all five matches; he was top of both the batting and bowling averages. But he was not allowed to captain Yorkshire. There sat Lord Hawke, solid and immutable, safer on his throne than Queen Victoria was on hers, and, it seemed, likely to be in occupation for as long.

There were other captains, often successful because of their idiosyncracies. Warwick Armstrong, the Australian behemoth, spent the journey from Australia to England shovelling coal into the ship's boilers to keep his weight down; he read an evening newspaper while fielding on the boundary in the Test Match at the Oval, and, it was generally understood, picked the England team to play against him. For it was rumoured that if he knew his batsmen could master a certain bowler, then that bowler was allowed to bowl out the Australians in a county match, and, similarly, a batsman whom they felt they could dismiss cheaply, was given a hundred runs. Naturally, Armstrong's team won the Test Series without defeat.

Douglas Jardine, resplendent in his Harlequin cap, unleashed Bodyline Bowling; temporarily blunted Bradman's genius; ignored the larrikins who cursed and spat at him; won the Test Series in Australia, and came nearer to dismantling the British Empire than either Kaiser Bill before him or Adolf Hitler after.

Arthur Carr, captain of Nottinghamshire and England, based his success on seeing that his fast bowlers got a plentiful supply of beer.

The Honourable Lionel Tennyson, grandson of Alfred Lord Tennyson, Poet Laureate, captain of Hampshire and England, batting almost one-handed because of injury, scored 36 and 63 against the Australians at Leeds. Once, batting against Yorkshire and finding all his fierce drives intercepted, he was enjoined by a stentorian voice from the boundary – 'Tha wants to read t'fielders one o' thi grandfather's poems. *That'll* send 'em to sleep.'

I myself, at a very early age, was a self-appointed captain. When I was a little boy I was the only one in our street who possessed a cricket bat. As soon as we had chosen teams, I naturally proposed myself as captain. Because my

The Hon. Lionel Tennyson (the Poet Laureate's grandson) batting one-handed against the Australians at Headingley in 1921. He scored 36 and 63.

11

accomplishments with both bat and ball were minimal, this appointment was loudly condemned. Nevertheless, after I had taken my bat home two or three times, my permanent elevation to that office was tacitly accepted. And, of course, knowing the rights of my authority, even as a child, I always batted first and bowled first.

My first task as captain was to win the toss and this I took it upon myself to do. Pure mathematicians, from the pinnacle of their Einsteinian universe, will tell you that the probability of winning the toss is given by the formula, $p^n + {}^nC_1 p^{n-1} q^1 + {}^nC_2 p^{n-2} q^2 + \ldots q^n$ which gives the various probabilities in $(H + T)$ tosses, where $p = q = \frac{1}{2}$, and H = Heads and T = Tails.

Stripped of its jargon this means 'fifty-fifty', but such unsatisfactory odds were not good enough for three of us – Lord Hawke, Dr. W. G. Grace and myself.

Lord Hawke, as he perambulated on his tours to the far-flung outposts of the Empire, would proffer to the colonial opposing him an English coin of the realm with Victoria on one side and Britannia on the other.

As the coin was in the air Lord Hawke called *'Woman'*. And when it descended, whichever way it fell, 'Woman', of course, it was. And as Lord Hawke abjured the modern nonsensicality of giving his opponents first innings, he always added, 'We'll bat'.

Dr. Grace, who believed in winning irrespective of umpires or laws of the game, was addicted to a similar ploy. As the coin was tossed into the air he called, 'It's a monkey'. Then, hardly deigning to glance at it as it rested on the ground, he added, 'And a monkey it is! We'll bat first.'

My own foray into this facet of captaincy had, necessarily, to follow a different pattern. We had no money. We received sixpence a week pocket money of which threepence went immediately into the Yorkshire Penny Bank and the other threepence was spent on peas and pies and a bottle of pop at the Sunday school social on the Saturday evening.

So we chose innings by tossing the bat in the air with a twisting motion. The face of the bat was flat, the back humped, so, as it circled in the air, we called 'Hump' or 'Hollow' according to our fancy as to which side would alight uppermost.

And here, long before it was recognised as such by insurance companies and high pressure advertising agencies, I made my first excursion into the science of statistics. Taking my bat into the garden one evening I made a hundred tosses and noted which way it fell. It was not an experiment fraught with pleasure. For half-way through, my father looked out of the window, saw me at my problem, came out and clouted me across the earhole. 'Thou'rt bahn to break that new bat', he said and, returning to the house, announced to my mother, 'I'm sure that lad of ours is barmy.'

But after he had gone on his nightly jaunt to the Working Men's Club I was able to complete my research and found the bat came down 'Hump' 68 times.

Thereafter I always called 'Hump', won the toss for my side and batted first. In this, of course, I followed the practice of Lord Hawke, but not for the same reason. His lordship took first innings because he feared that the rain and the wear and tear of studs might damage the pitch: we played on the setts in the back street, a strip that neither rain nor shine could harm.

But while our game might be impervious to the idiosyncracies of the weather, it

'Tossing up.'

was not immune from my mother. Half-way through the match she would come to our garden gate and shout, 'Harry, I want thee to go to t' Co-op for me.' And in those halcyon days children obeyed their parents.

So, having had my innings of course, I seized my bat and went home, leaving my team-mates and opponents to play 'tip cat', 'tin can squats out', or 'hinkum, jinkum, jerryman, buck'.

In 1924 Arthur Gilligan was appointed captain of England in the Test Series against South Africa. In the opening match at Edgbaston he put himself on first, took six wickets for seven runs and bowled South Africa out for 30. But Cecil Parkin, the mercurial Lancastrian born within spitting distance of the Yorkshire boundary, was in the England team. And Cecil considered himself the premier bowler in England. So while the critics lauded Gilligan, Parkin complained bitterly that he should have opened the bowling and vowed never to play for England again.

In the Golden Era of cricket, before Kaiser Bill had destroyed for ever humour and indulgence and when gentlemen of leisure abounded, C. B. Fry brought his Sussex team to play a northern county. In those days the southern counties often contained a preponderance of amateurs in gaudy caps and blazers that would have shamed Joseph's coat, and usually their ability was in inverse ratio to the magnificence of their attire.

A northern spectator, no doubt a woolsorter or weaving overlooker from Huddersfield, having spent the whole of the morning refreshing himself in the ale

'Nobbut a bloody professional . . .' C. B. Fry.

tent, sat out the rest of the day in the sun, announcing loudly, 'Fry, Fry, ye amateurs is no bloody good.'

But Fry, as usual, made a huge score, whereupon the enraged spectator, after another sojourn in the ale tent, spent the rest of the match bawling, 'Fry, Fry, thou'rt nowt nobbut a bloody professional thisen.'

Seeing that he cannot please everybody, it is much wiser if the captain attempts to please nobody but himself, that he rules as a demigod following his own idiosyncracies and inclinations wherever they may point, and however outrageous they may be.

Village cricket captains have always done this. When the West Riding professional clubs began to spread their wings and import internationals from distant climes, there was a feeling, momentarily, that these world famous, expensive additions, some of whom had driven Test Selection Committees to distraction with their prima donna tantrums, might overawe a village lad who worked in the mill and lived in a chamber-height cottage in the chapel fold.

One, a dusky son of another hemisphere, arrived from a sunny clime to play his first match on a West Riding hilltop with a smell of snow still in the bitter April wind.

His stiff, frozen fingers could not control the ball and in his first three overs he was unceremoniously thumped for 20 runs. Regardless of his world-wide reputation, the captain told him to put his sweater on. 'And where do you want me to field, skipper?' he inquired politely. The captain looked at his expensive acquisition with loathing. 'In t'bloody pavilion for all t'good thou art', he retorted bitterly.

Another, in consultation with his captain, before the first over, set his field with micrometer precision. But a couple of balls strayed down the leg side and were flicked away for runs. Before his next over, the professional asked third slip to move to square leg. Looking up, the captain observed the fielder and inquired where he was going. On being told of the professional's decision, the captain ordered the fielder back to slip and approached the professional. 'Tha's set thi field once', he said. 'Nah bowl to it and stop beggaring 'em abaht'.

There was, 40 or 50 years ago, a sort of Racial Discrimination in reverse. Leary Constantine had been such an outstanding success at Nelson and such an attraction in the Lancashire League that other clubs tried to jump on the band waggon. So much so that an unsuccessful English professional often had to suffer the jibe, 'If tha expects anybody to pay thee next season tha'll have to blacken thi face.'

But not every West Indian was a Constantine and some did not find it easy to mix and be accepted by the insular, self-centred, parochial West Riding villagers.

One, entering the ale tent after his first match, was accosted by a veteran in an attempt to put him at his ease.

'And where does tha come from lad?" asked the supporter.

'From the Bahamas, man', smiled the West Indian.

The veteran, for whom, probably, the world began at Blackpool and ended at Scarborough, looked wisely at the supple, boneless figure 'Aye', he nodded sagely after a long inspection, 'I understand. Tha looks varry much like a banana thisen.'

But if their playing ability did not always match their reputation, they quickly learned the Yorkshire proverb that 'Ony fooil can spend brass.'

One West Indian, going into the bar after a match, saw in front of him a new acquisition – all sparkling glass, shining chromium and gaudy paint.

'What is this?' he asked a member.

'It's a fruit machine', he was told.

'And what do you do?' he inquired.

'Well', said the member, 'tha puts a penny in that slot and pulls t'handle. And sometimes tha gets twopence back and sometimes fourpence.'

'Ah', said the West Indian joyfully, 'that's for me, man.'

He was just about to insert his penny when the member added, as a sort of afterthought, 'Of course, sometimes tha gets nowt'.

The West Indian looked at him in disbelief, then pocketed his penny.

Even when successful, the West Indian was not appreciated by everybody. One, signed in the middle '30s for the fee (exorbitant then) of £6 a match, was taking a lot of wickets. His club, faced with this mammoth expenditure, had little money left, but to complement him at the other end, they managed to afford a veteran bowler long past his prime, running to fat and seed, who, after bowling 20 overs, was utterly exhausted.

After one long hot, Saturday evening stint, the veteran sat disconsolate and disillusioned in the dressing room. The West Indian, silk shirt gleaming, wide-brimmed hat jauntily askew, bade his team-mates 'Good evening', without a sign of exhaustion or even perspiration. But the veteran still sat hunched, a towel round his sagging shoulders, a fag end hanging moistly from his lips. His greying hair was wet and rumpled.

A crony of the veteran came into the dressing tent, smacked him cheerfully on the back, and, in that encouraging way, so typical of Yorkshiremen, said, 'Tha aren't doing so well this season, Billy!'

Stung to aggression the veteran looked up. 'How the 'ell's tha mean? Ah'm doing better than *that* black bugger.'

'Nay, Billy', admonished his crony, 'he's taken six wickets today. Thou's nobbut getten two.'

'Aye', snarled the outraged veteran, *'he's* getten six wickets for £6. *I've* getten two for thirty bob.'

But whether in sunshine or shadow, success or failure, the West Indian professionals were always perfect gentlemen, polite, considerate, helpful. During the war a village club on the outskirts of Huddersfield arranged a benefit match for its members in the Forces. An array of international and county men agreed to play, among them E. A. (Manny) Martindale, the West Indian Test Match fast bowler.

After the match, the club secretary, knowing that some professionals, even in benefit matches, demanded their expenses, went amongst them asking how much they wanted. Of those who had played, Martindale had travelled the farthest, from Lancashire, at a time when petrol was severely rationed, train services were curtailed, and when he would have to put up at an hotel for the night.

To the first player the secretary said, 'Nah then, Teddy, how much do we owe thee?'

The player looked round and, aware that Martindale would be most out of pocket, said, 'Nay, Ah don't knaw. Give me t'same as thou'rt giving Manny.'

The second player, asked the same question, replied, 'Oh, give me t'same as thou'rt giving Teddy.'

Thereupon Martindale was approached. 'I've enjoyed myself enormously', he smiled in delight. 'I don't want a penny. I never charge expenses for matches for players in the Forces.' There is at least one middle-aged man walking about in the West Riding blessed with the Christian name Emmanuel because of his father's understandable hero-worship of Martindale.

I was initiated into a captain's duties at an early age. As a very young man, probably because my prospective father-in-law was on the selection committee, I was chosen as vice-captain of a professional league team. Our captain, Vernon, was a veteran of much experience, wise in the ways of cricket.

When he fielded, he opened with his professional bowlers, but they got nobody out. He replaced them with his amateurs who were no more successful, whereupon he brought back his professionals, still with no benefit. Weekly our opponents scored about 250 runs, declared, with five or six wickets down, and beat us by round about 100 runs. Soon we were bottom of the league.

But one week Vernon was ill and I, full of trepidation, was promoted in his place. Not daring to deviate from Vernon's classical approach, I opened with our professional bowlers. But this time, surprisingly, they bowled one or two out. I gave them a rest and brought on the amateurs. They, too, took wickets and soon the professionals were back to polish off the tail end. Our opponents were all out for 103.

As we were going off the field an ancient supporter came and clapped me on the shoulder. 'Harry, lad', he said, almost with tears in his eyes, 'that's what we've been short of all t'season. A captain that knew hah to handle his bowlers.'

MORE CAPTAINS

The roll of Yorkshire cricket captains is not long. In the mists of antiquity they had professional captains. In 1876 and 1877 it was Ephraim Lockwood, known to his intimates as 'Mary Ann'. Eph was a Yorkshireman from the Pennine Hills with all a Yorkshireman's love of his county. In 1879 he toured Canada with Richard Daft's team, and, as a special treat, was taken to see Niagara Falls. When asked if he was impressed, Eph, homesick, replied, 'It's all reyt in its way. But Ah'd rayther be starin' at t'beck at Holmfirth.'

He was followed for five years by Tom Emmett. You will not find Tom's name among the champions of cricket for run-scoring or wicket-taking, but Tom has one record to his credit, or discredit. He bowled more wides than anyone else who ever played first class cricket – averaging 50 a year for 20 years, and not many cricketers can boast, or admit, to having bowled over 1,000 wides. He also told W. G. Grace, after one enormous innings, 'They ought to mak' thee bat with a littler bat.'

But the days of these jolly, professional captains were numbered. In 1883 the Hon. Martin Hawke, soon to become Lord Hawke, assumed the captaincy and for 28 years was an autocratic figurehead – in reality a hydra-headed dictator, for during the second half of his captaincy he was also the president of the Yorkshire County Cricket Club, and remained so until his death in 1938.

He took as his model of government the Kingdom of Heaven, with himself as Jehovah and George Hirst bearing the Ark of the Covenant.

Lord Hawke – 'a hydra-headed dictator'.

Almost immediately the team was enormously successful, as was only to be expected, because, as everyone except the politicians knows, a dictatorship is superior to a democracy.

It was a regime that would have been appreciated by the Israelites wandering in Sinai, for a dropped catch was frowned upon by Lord Hawke as severely as Moses regarded the Golden Calf.

During his reign, three players, two of them the outstanding left-arm bowlers of their generation, were summarily dismissed from the team, one, at least, for appearing on the field in a cheerfully inebriated condition.

Lord Hawke was followed by a few military and ennobled men, cricket nonentities, so that, for all practical purposes, Yorkshire played with ten men. But one of them, at least, satisfied Wilfred Rhodes's keen judgement. 'He wor a good captain', said Wilfred when asked his opinion. 'He allus did as Ah telled him.' Another was not so easily coerced, so Wilfred, when he felt it was time he was put on to bowl, would walk about in front of him, ruffling his sweater up and down as a broad hint that it was high time he took it off.

Probably these appointed gentlemen captained their men as they had done the P.B.I. on the Somme, fearlessly, gallantly, but requiring a 'sir' at the end of every statement and impervious to criticism or advice.

But the piratical crew who, in those days, made up Yorkshire's incomparable team had their own means of showing their displeasure at any decision that they felt had militated against their quick success. In those days the amateurs had their own dressing room and their own gate from which to enter the field. If the captain had annoyed the professionals, they stayed in their own room and allowed him to occupy the field, alone, before 20,000 spectators. At last one of them, and if it were not Wilfred it must surely have been Emmott Robinson, would say, 'He's stood theer on his own makkin' an exhibition of hissen long enough. We might as weel go aht an' join him nah.'

Egalitarianism succeeded privilege in the world. Two fine young captains, A. T. Barber in 1930 and F. E. Greenwood in 1931 and 1932 occupied the post, but they, like so many young men of the post-First World War era, found that the world did not automatically provide them with a living, nor did they, like so many young men after the Second World War, feel that it owed them one. They departed to business.

They were followed by Brian Sellers in 1933 – mighty both in physique and valour, a man born out of his time, a man, who, in an earlier generation, with arm and voice, would have hurled Caesar's hordes from our Brigantian kingdom or outmatched Henry VIII as the premier athlete of his day.

His father, Arthur, had also played for Yorkshire in his day and had been given a lesson by the great W. G. Grace himself on the value of money. The Doctor had reached his century (whether in the number of hundreds scored, in age, or in the number of patients lost I cannot say) and a national newspaper was giving him, in spite of the amateur status he professed, a shilling for every run he scored in the rest of the season. Batting together in one match, he and Arthur were making light work of some weak bowling, Sellers outmatching the Doctor both in runs and style. At last the Doctor's patience was exhausted. He strode across the wicket.

Above F. E. Greenwood.

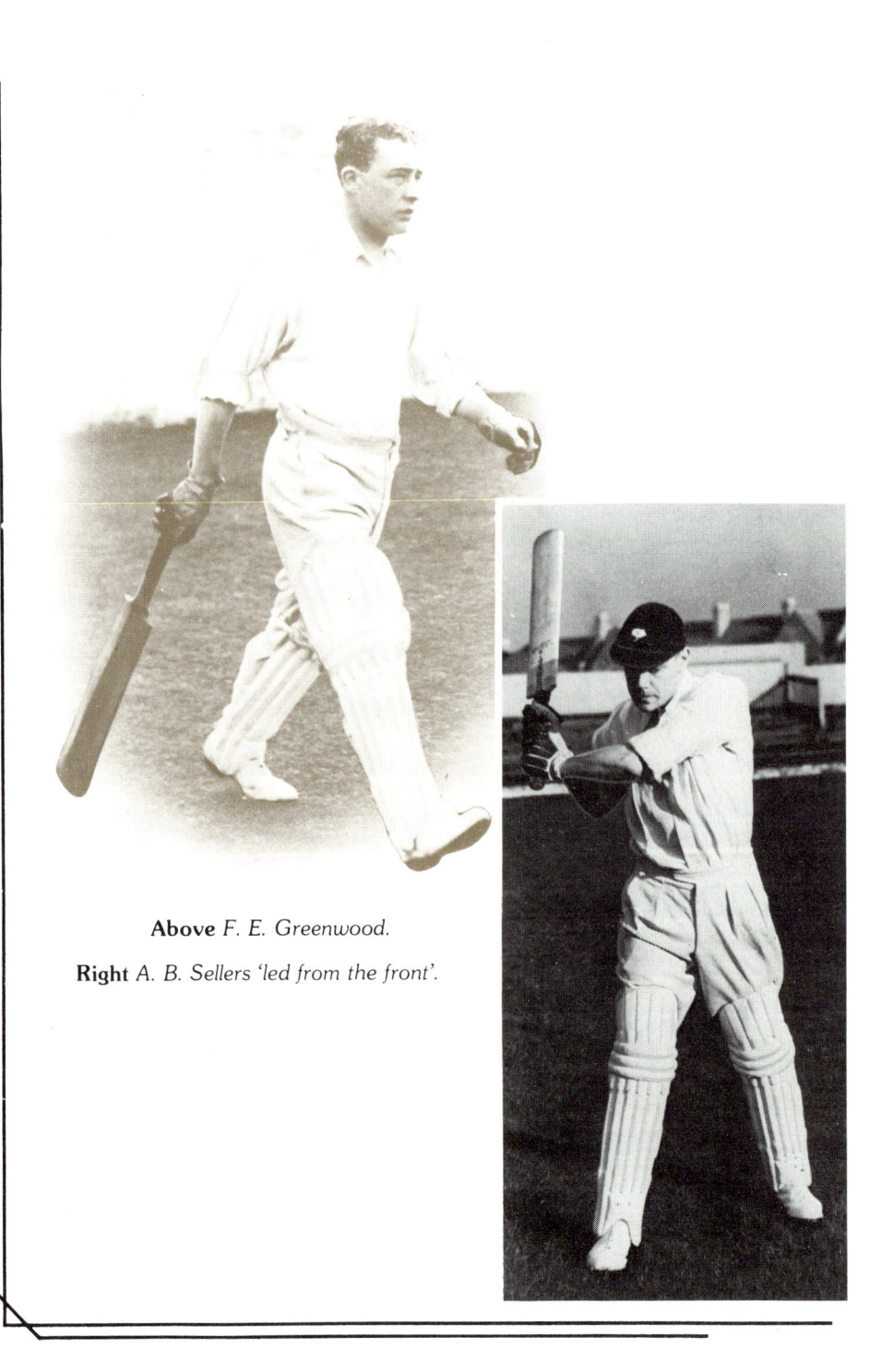

Right A. B. Sellers 'led from the front'.

'Arthur', he said in annoyance, 'don't you know I'm getting a shilling a run. Quieten down and let me do the scoring.'

But W. G.'s avarice did not infect Arthur. When Brian, as a very young man, scored his first fifty and, joyously, took his collection home, Arthur congratulated him warmly and then said (for this was in the days before the National Health Service made hypochondriacs of us all), 'First thing tomorrow morning you must take it to the matron at Keighley Victoria Hospital.'

Brian would have delighted Napoleon. Like Buonaparte's marshals, he led from the front. He could, when necessary, show a plebeian forthrightness and if a man creates his own luck, then Brian was a lucky man. In the seven years up to the war, when he captained them, Yorkshire were champions five times. He returned after the war for two years, winning the championship again in 1946, but age and war had decimated his forces. Not till 1959 were they to win it again outright, and by this time the age of distinction between Gentlemen and Players was ending. All, from now on, were cricketers, and all, presumably, accepted the emoluments which resulted from turning sport into a high pressure business.

In this country, the easiest team to captain should be England. Given the six best batsmen and the four best bowlers in the land, it should be impossible to go wrong.

The strategists and theorists, who discuss opening batsmen, middle order batsmen, swing, seam and spin bowlers, are merely creating problems where none exist.

Good batsmen can score runs wherever they go in. When I was a little lad in short pants I had the honour to score for our Sunday school cricket team. Before our innings I would approach the captain with the score book and ask for the batting order. If we had lost the week before, he would look at me quizzically and then say, 'Put me down t'last as usual. Then change all t'rest round from last Saturday.' We still scored about the same number of runs, but the unkind speculation that this was probably because all were as bad as each other was refuted by England in the Test Match at Adelaide in January, 1925.

Due to some nonsense about 'night watchmen', Jack Hobbs went in at number 5, Herbert Sutcliffe at 7 and Pat Hendren 8. But Hobbs scored 119, Sutcliffe 33 and Hendren 92 in a total of 365 – more than was scored in the second innings when they batted in the 'correct' order. Nor does it matter much which bat they pick up in the pavilion. Victor Trumper, the great Australian stylist, who, by his eminence C. B. Fry was rated, with Grace, Ranjitsinjhi and Bradman, among the four greatest-ever batsmen, was going out to bat in an Inter-State match. As he walked to the wicket, a little lad ran on to the field carrying his own childish bat. 'Mr. Trumper,' he asked eagerly, "will you please bat with my bat today?' So Victor swapped bats with the child and still scored over 50.

And anyone, on occasion, can take a wicket. Lord Hawke took one (though only one) in his 28 years as captain of Yorkshire.

Ronnie Burnet took one. He was in his fortieth year when, as a disciplinary measure, he was appointed captain of Yorkshire in 1958. A Roses match was dying on its feet. It was the last day. A draw was a foregone conclusion. The players were gently going through the motions till, thankfully, the umpires called 'Time, gentlemen, please'.

Ranjitsinjhi – 'one of the four greatest batsmen'.

Whimsically Burnet decided to bowl himself; perhaps he felt a little comedy would brighten up the deadly situation. But he produced the most glorious slow leg break. Baffled and bewildered, the Lancashire batsman, Booth, groped bemusedly to find its flight, lost it and stretched wretchedly down the pitch before being bowled neck and crop. If Burnet could have produced one of these an over, instead, alas, of one in a career, he would have won Test Matches for England instead of guiding Yorkshire to a Championship title in 1959 and then retiring.

Who else, besides Lord Hawke and Ronnie Burnet, took just one wicket for Yorkshire? Well, there were Percy Holmes, the magnificent opening bat for 20 years, Arthur Dolphin, stumper for 18 years, the palindromically named Sir K. Lister-Kaye, and W. Wordsworth – not the one who saw the 'host of golden daffodils'.

And in 1979, if Geoff Boycott had taken the one more wicket required to qualify, he would have topped the All England bowling averages. But Boycott is an excellent bowler, and if he had loved bowling as much as Wilfred Rhodes loved batting, he might have been as great an all-rounder.

CAPTAIN, MY CAPTAIN

Test and County captains have no idea of the doubts and difficulties that beset the captain of a village cricket club. With assistance from selectors, chairmen, managers and members, and advice and instruction from newspaper columnists, critics and experts they simply have to toss up, write down the batting order and change the bowling when the mood takes them.

A village cricket captain's duties, however, start two hours before the match. He has to open up the tea tent, take out all the forms that have been stored there during the week and set them round the field, carefully avoiding the north-east corner (where the sneaking wind from the moor comes after tea, threatening bronchitis and pleurisy to the veterans) and avoiding also the spot where the reek from the farmyard muck heap suffuses the field when the sun is hot.

Then he must sweep out the tea tent, for you cannot expect ladies in their best summer frocks and colourful aprons to do that, covering themselves with dust at the very start of the afternoon.

He must light the Heath-Robinson contraption of a tea urn, for it 'plops' thunderously and frightens the ladies, who therefore hold the taper so far away that the gas would never ignite.

Then there is the boundary tape to be run out, a pot of whitewash to be mixed, the creases marked and a rolling team assembled before the match can begin.

Twenty minutes before starting time a little lad will come into the field and announce, 'Mi mother's sent me to tell you she won't let mi father laik today. She's makking him tak' us to Blackpool for hawf a day. She says she's stalled o' sticking in t' house ivery Set'day while he laiks cricket. So you'll hev to find somebody else or laik with ten men', and then a self-satisfied seventeen-year-old member of the team will approach him. 'Oh, Edwin', he will say casually, as if the welfare of the team is of little importance, 'I'm taking a bird to a disco tonight and I've arranged to meet her at six o'clock. If we field first, thou'll hev to let me go in first when we bat or I shall miss my innings. She's a right smart bit o' stuff and if tha won't let me . . .' But Edwin interrupts his eulogy. 'Aye', he says, 'all reyt. Ah'll see tha goes in t'first', before bending again to his boundary tape and muttering 'Daft young bugger' to himself.

One village captain, a good batsman, always went in first when they played away, and last at home. When I mentioned his idiosyncracy to him, he said, 'Has thou also noticed that when we laik at home we allus bat t'first? I don't win t'toss every week. I agree it with t'other captain. Thou sees, we can nobbut get three women to help us and they spend all their time buttering t'sandwiches and setting out t'cups and plates, so there's nobody left but me to sell t'ice cream. If we fielded first or I went in and scored a lot o'runs it'd all hev melted by t'time Ah got back, because we haven't a fridge. So, tha sees, Ah'm forced to go in t'last.'

And now comes the captain's most important consultation. Across to the tea tent he goes and, metaphorically, doffs his cap in front of the lady in charge. She looks at him thoughtfully and considers for a minute. 'Ah'm going to t'bingo tonight', she says, 'and eyes down is at six o'clock. So I want this place shut up by hawf-past five. Arrange for t'interval at quarter-past four.'

Meekly he backs out and goes into solemn conclave with the visiting captain.

Irrespective of the state of the game, the declaration time is agreed upon. Irrespective of who ultimately wins, the band has been kept 'in the nick'.

And then, just before the match starts he has to dash down to the joiner's for a bag of sawdust, return to welcome the umpires and prepare to satisfy the ancients who, puffing their pipes, will have nothing but ridicule for the efforts of the modern generation.

Usually the match finishes about seven o'clock, but, for the captain, the day is not yet over. There will come a call from the tea tent, 'Edwin can you come and give us a hand to finish the washing up. We've getten a bit behind-hand'. Then will come a call from a departing player, 'Edwin, don't forget to pay the umpires'.

The boundary tapes have to be got in, the benches stored, the pitch given a run up and down with the light roller. The gas has to be turned off; the shutters put up.

Wearily, long after the rest, he wanders home and opens the door. There, arms akimbo, stands his wife. 'Tha's been drinking in t'pub instead o' comin' home ageean', she complains shrilly. And as he attempts to justify his lateness, she continues, 'Tha *must* have been. It's an hour since Ah saw Tom Greenwood going down t'street with his cricket bag, and tha tells me he's your last man in. If tha thinks Ah'm bahn to sit here twiddling mi thumbs ivvery Set'day neet while tha goes drinking afore tha's t'decency to come home . . .'

He mashes himself a pot of tea and slumps in his chair. 'By Gow', he sighs, 'but Ah'll resign from this bloody job at t'end of t'season.'

But, of course, when the annual meeting comes round, he does nothing of the sort. What does a divorce matter as long as he can carry on as captain of the village club?

TALES FROM THE ALE TENT

It has ever been the mark of a servile people that they ape their superiors, and in no phase of living is this more evident than in architecture. After William, with his Norman followers and Picardian mercenaries, had spurned the English resistance and impressed his sovereignty on his cowering foes, his rapturous adventures proclaimed their mastery by covering the southern shires with an orgasm of castle building.

Machiolation, tympanum, spandrel, tracery, in splendorous confusion, pronounced the domination of the Norman; and the conquered southerners, peering shyly from their rude hovels in the forest, deemed these monstrosities of ornamentation good, and determined to follow the examples of their overlords.

This glorification of decoration bit deep into the soul, and when cricket emerged as civilisation's greatest single advance since Grecian culture, man erected round his fields pavilions and marquees, gaudy and decorative with false battlement, flying buttress and gay pennant, till the game degenerated to a mime in a Field of Cloth of Gold.

But not in the Yorkshire Pennines! Here, on an irregularly contoured, undulating hillside bounded by dry stone walls and greasy becks, the Northman flattened out a strip in the middle, and, in clogs and homespun worsted, batted and bowled from morn till night while spiders spun their webs on the framework of his handloom and the sunbeams, slanting through his garret window, danced on the dust settling on warp and spindle.

Presumably he mastered the art of bat and ball to the detriment of his craft of weaving. At any rate, while the world rang with admiration of his cricket, it grumbled disgustedly that 'Three great evils come out of the North – a cold wind, a cunning knave and a shrinking cloth.' Unconcerned, he decided to erect in his field, for the necessities and decencies of human life, three huts, which should be known as the Dressing Tent, the Ale Tent and the Tea Tent.

There must be no attempt at ornamentation of these wooden structures. Low and squat, four-square to the wind, like a Pennine hill farm, daubed hideously with creosote, each is built and situated to the greatest advantage of the cricket club.

The dressing tent is carefully badly constructed, and stuck in the draughtiest corner where the wind from the mountain clough sweeps like a torrent round Cape Horn. The window frames are ill-fitting, the floor is splintered and unplaned. The latchless door swings wide and an upthrust shutter, socketed with an iron bar into the frame, allows the Atlantic gales to howl like an imp in the cold, damp shed.

'We build t'dressing tent uncomfortable like', a president explained proudly, 'then they'll get out to practise as sharp as they can and won't stop in telling tales and smoking cigarettes all t'evening.'

The ale tent is a different matter. The man who sits and drinks his beer is, at least in theory, more important than those who merely play, or the woman who stands and washes up. The ale tent must be built with the most commanding view of the play, and the side facing the game must glisten with glass like a greenhouse.

The window will be covered with narrow wire mesh and a fortnight's staring through them will convert every member into a myope. But the National Health will provide free spectacles, for every member will be able to prove that the disability is an industrial ailment caused by peering too intently at the close weave of fine worsteds in their employment as warp dressers, textile overlookers or wool combers.

The solvency of the cricket club depends on the supping of ale, and if the club is to survive, the tent must be made as congenial as the tap room of the local pub.

A stove, glowing like a brick kiln, occupies the centre. Round, inlaid tables with decorated cast iron legs, are strewn about. There are dart boards, dominoes, cribbage markers and spittoons in profusion.

The walls are covered with faded photographs of teams of long ago; long-moustached, cloth-capped, reclining like ballet dancers round a cup or shield, with a line of officials at the back in blue serge and billycocks with gold alberts swinging over their ample middles.

The ale tent is the glory of the cricket club. Over their pints the veterans sit and recall, with chuckle and anecdote, games of yester-year. 'Does tha remember in 1899', says one, 'when Amos were t'captain, and that new professional from London who said he'd laiked in Test Matches dropped two catches? Amos took t'ball off him and went on to bowl hissen. He set all his fielders except t'professional. "Where would you like me to go?" says t'professional. "Into t'tea tent helping t'women", says Amos. "But if thou did, thou'd only drop t'cups." '

There is a fusillade of laughter and spluttering coughs. More pints are ordered; and where is there a better place to drink a glass of ale than in a cricket tent with, before you, the ground where your youthful glories were enacted, and sitting round you, or staring down at you from their yellow photographs, the pals who shared your joys and heartaches?

Near midnight, for no well-brought up Pennine bobby would dream of enforcing statutory closing hours at the cricket club, the ancients, rheumaticky and stiff, tap their way to the gate.

'Good night, lad', and, 'Thee be careful crossing t'moor', they bid each other as they separate, each, in the words of the old North-country poem,

Toddling home to the fireside bliss,
  Toddling home to the childer's kiss,
God bless yond bit of curling smoke,
  God bless yond cosy chimney nook,
I'm fain to be toddling home.

Village cricket clubs have always been aware that the laws of the land, particularly the licensing laws, did not apply to them, or, at least, they did not until these sorry, recent days when the ale tent has been euphemistically re-named the 'club house' with bingo drives every evening and strip shows at Sunday lunch-time.

Quickly, in my youth, I was made aware of this disregard for legalism. Much to the disgust and dismay of my mother's chapel-going lady friends (who, with countenances as woeful as the Witch of Endor's, predicted for me an inevitable sorry end) I had joined a professional club.

Practice nights were Tuesday and Thursday, but I did not practise long. We batted ten minutes, bowled ten minutes and then retired to the ale tent to join a game of ha'penny pontoon.

Long after dark we played, the card school growing to a dozen or more, with the kitty piled high on the ornate cast-iron legged table. When I returned home long past eleven o'clock, my father would say, 'By gow, thou'rt late toneet'. But I had only to reply, 'Aye, we were discussing tactics with an old member' for him to go happily to bed.

One Tuesday night, long after the steward should have called 'time', the door was pushed open and a bobby walked in. Pints of ale were on every table, the tent was full of bibulous men, froth spilled from the bar. And my world tumbled about me. Prosecuted for drinking after hours, I should be case out by my parents, disgraced at the Sunday school and expelled from my grammar school!

Pushing past the bobby, I shot out of the door, bolted across the fields, jumped on a tram, and, as calmly as my pounding heart would allow, went home and straight to bed before my father could question me. On Wednesday and Thursday evening, as soon as the paper arrived, I searched every page for news of the raid, but nothing was reported.

When I went to Thursday practice I went into the ale tent and poked a somnolent member in the ribs. He awoke with a start. 'What happened on Tuesday neet?' I asked anxiously. 'Tuesday neet?' he said. 'Wheer, lad?' 'In here', I said. Again he looked at me and pondered. 'Nay, nowt out of t'ordinary that I knaw abaht', he finally opined.

'But', I insisted, 'a policeman came in twenty minutes after closing time and they were still serving ale'.

His face lit up with understanding, 'Oh, *him*', he said. 'He allus calls in abaht that time for a couple of pints when he's on t'neet shift.'

Once, in the distant past, a small market town had been granted the honour of a Yorkshire Second Team match in the Minor Counties Competition. The match was of two days' duration, playing hours were from eleven o'clock till seven, with a luncheon interval from 1.30 till 2.15.

Alas, the ale tent licence did not allow them to open till 2.30, so that the army of spectators that was expected to grace the event faced the dire prospect of a 'dry' lunch.

And so, at a special meeting it was decided that the chairman and secretary of the cricket club should approach the sergeant in charge of the local police station with a view to getting a special dispensation for the two days of the match.

'Nay', said the sergeant when they explained their dilemma, 'Ah can't do that. Nobbut t'Watch Committee can alter t'licensing hours and they haven't another meeting for a month.' He studied for a moment and then added, 'But I'll tell you what I *will* do: I've nobbut two bobbies – I'll send one on point duty on t'cross roads on t'moors. There's nobbut abaht one motor-car an hour passes but I'll order him to stop there from twelve o'clock till three; and t'other can go and investigate a case of dogs worrying sheep reyt up on t'edge. It'll take him an hour's walk to get there and another hour back.'

'But what if t'chairman of t'Watch Committee comes to t'match?' asked the anxious secretary.

'Him?' said the sergeant. 'If he sees t'bar open he'll be t'first in for a pint.'

HEROINES OF THE TEA TENT

During the last few years there has evolved an hilarious Quango, the Equal Opportunities Commission. You may no longer advertise for a groundsman. Unless you wish to suffer the utmost rigours of the law you must, I suppose, define your requirement as 'a groundsman (ess)' or a grounds-person. However, an equally stern emanation from the Commission for Racial Equality would make it unwise for a foundry requiring a blacksmith to ask for a blackperson or describe a tinsmith as a whiteperson.

Fortunately, with careful improvisation such difficulties are not insurmountable. A riding establishment requiring a stable lad shrank from so obviously exposing itself to the severity of British justice. Instead, it invited applications for the post of stable hand, adding, 'The successful applicant will be required to sleep in the caravan with the stable jockey on journeys to race meetings.'

Cricket, fortunately for its players, has so far ignored the effusions of HM Government — with complete immunity, or so it would appear.

Blatantly, it advertises a reward for the 'Man of the Match', and so some player who has scored runs, taken wickets, or bestirred himself in the field, is given a trophy or a handsome cheque. Luckily for him, the letter of the modern law is not obeyed and the prize is not offered for the *Person* of the Match. For in that case the prize would always go to some lady who had slaved away the sunny Saturday afternoon, mashing tea and cutting sandwiches to fortify those taking a little gentle exercise on the rich green meadow under God's blue firmament.

And later, when the senior players have departed to their ale and the younger ones to the company of their belles, the tea tent ladies face yet another hour's labour washing up greasy plates, scalding out the tea urn and wringing out dishclothes. As they wend their weary way home, they are greeted by a complaining 'By gum, t'potted meat in your sandwiches were a bit off today. Wor it some you had left over from t'Darby and Joan Club on Thursday afternoon?' This from some ancient tippler seeking a breath of fresh air before returning for another pint.

Unsung, the ladies slave and sweat in their cubby-holes and, even there, sometimes, are at the whims of their lords and masters. Bursting into the tea tent one Saturday afternoon as the players were coming off the field for the interval, the home captain, his face livid with anger, shouted, 'Mary! Mary!' Startled, his wife came timidly from her buttering. 'Tha sees that umpire — that tall 'un with t'black moustache? He's given seven of our lads out leg before wicket today. See tha doesn't put much boiled ham in *his* sandwiches!'

But at least one young West Riding lady had cause to bless the day she decided to devote her Saturday afternoons to the welfare of cricketers.

She had applied for admission to a southern university, and, on arrival for interview, was told that instead of a mere lecturer to see her, the professor himself required her attendance.

Trembling, she was brought into his presence. Quickly, he ordered the usher to leave and shut the door.

The professor, a Heckmondwike man who had wasted his life and academic abilities in southern climes and his Saturdays on the effete cricket fields south of the River Trent, secretly pined for his homeland.

In mock severity he looked at the frightened applicant, then picked up her form. 'It says here you come from Cleckheaton.' She nodded in agreement and he added, 'Do you help in t'tea tent at Hartshead Moor cricket club?'

'No', she smiled thinly, 'but I do at – 'and she mentioned one of those other delightful clubs – Spen Victoria, Hanging Heaton or Dewsbury and Savile, in the Heavy Woollen District.

He leapt up, embraced her, and pointed to the pile of application forms on his desk. 'Never mind about them', he laughed. 'Go home, lass, and get two A-levels and I'll accept thi in front of all that lot. And when tha reckons to be coming to me on a cold winter's neet for thi tutorial, we'll put another lump of coal on t'fire and Ah'll tell thi abaht George Hirst and Wilfred Rhodes and Len Hutton and Freddie Trueman.'

Unlike the ale tent, the unglamorous, utilitarian tea tent is built as far from the playing area as possible. An unbroken gable end faces the pitch. And it is here, – year in, year out – that mothers, wives and sweethearts mash countless pints of tea and cut and butter innumerable potted meat sandwiches.

They have to fetch the water in enamelled buckets from the farm kitchen three fields away: nothing to look at but the creeping docken under the crumbling dry stone wall where they empty the tea leaves; or the rows of trestle tables and gargantuan piles of unwashed crockery. But women know nothing of cricket and it would be a foolish risk to give them a window facing the play, for they would only gape and stare and neglect their duties, while understanding nothing of the high honour and skill of the contest.

And yet there have been Yorkshirewomen famous for their percipience both in the past and the present; for instance, Mother Skipton, one of whose little-known doggerel octets I quote –

When nineteen hundred suns have spun,
  The World the Northmen will have won.
Hawks will lead the leaping hounds,
  Conquerors on foreign grounds.
Lord de Trafford soon will yield
  To snow-white warriors in the field.
And Cantuar and bent ellipses
  Be undermined by cellar's witches.

Its elucidation defied the scholars, mystics and pundits of the Middle Ages, but to us it is clear. By 1900 Yorkshire was the world's foremost cricket team. 'Hawks leading leaping hounds' referred, of course, to Lord Hawke, as Yorkshire's captain, the hounds being his valiant team. 'Lord de Trafford' is Lord's and Old Trafford, where Yorkshire so often was victorious; and the snow-white warriors are the Yorkshire cricketers. Similarly, Cantuar and bent ellipses refer to the Kent County ground at Canterbury and Surrey's ground at the Oval, and surely, 'cellar's witches' are Brian Sellers and his band of pre war champions.

Both Churchill and Hitler envisaged their regimes lasting for 1,000 years. But Churchill has gone to his fathers, the British Empire to oblivion, and Hitler . . . On the death of Lloyd George the devil advised a fallen angel, sweltering and smouldering in Hell, to

Move a bit higher,
  Away from the fire
And make way for that liar, from Wales.

Surely, if that proved to be Lloyd George's ultimate destination, he also would move up a peg when Hitler was turned away from the Pearly Gates.

But in 1,000 years' time perhaps the most celebrated Yorkshirewoman will be Mollie Staines, for she was the first to breach the last stronghold of male chauvinism – she became a member of the Yorkshire County Cricket Committee.

The shades of John Ellison, J. B. Wolstinholm, George Padley, Lord Hawke, Sir

Frederick Toone, Major Lupton, Sir Archibald White, Roger Iddison and Joe Rowbotham must have spat their defiance, but Mollie was enthroned, to bring, perhaps, a gentler, sweeter touch to where, for 150 years, warriors had reigned unmolested.

Alas, perhaps in 1,000 years there will be neither male nor female, for the era of anonymity and unisex will be established. Only last season, sitting outside our Sunday school's dressing tent, awaiting a Methodist second team who were to play us, I watched the visitors turn in at the gate, a motley collection of youths and their girl friends, all with long hair, dark glasses, jeans and T-shirts. A veteran stared at them in disgust. 'T'trouble today is', he opined, 'thou can't tell one from t'other, unless t'lasses happens to be a bit busty.'

Surely, there will be cricket in Heaven. And in the seats of honour in the Royal

Mollie Staines 'breached the stronghold'.

*Troubled in Valhalla? M. J. Ellison (**right**) and J. B. Wostinholm (**far right**), one-time president and secretary respectively of the Yorkshire County Cricket Club.*

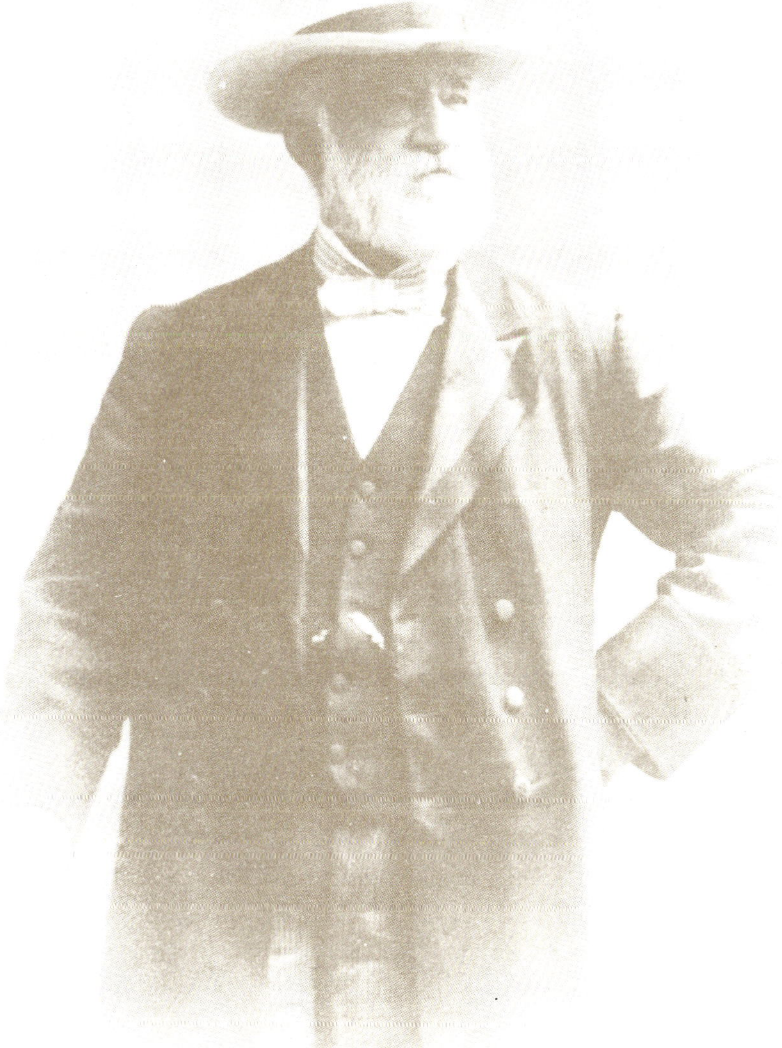

Pavilion, bedecked in their dazzling white splendour, will be the ladies of the tea tents. And who knows but that in the dungeons below, as near to Hades as can be, will be found Lord Hawke, Lord Harris, Dr. W. G. Grace, the Honourable Ivo Bligh, Sir Pelham Warner, Lord Dalmeny, the Honourable E. Chandos Leigh, the Earl of Bessborough, Viscount Ullswater and all, with aprons over their greasy wings, washing the dirty plates.

THEY ALSO SERVE

There are men playing regularly in Sunday school cricket whose career batting average is 0.33 runs per innings. There was, at the turn of the century, one who played for a village club in the Calder Valley of whom a colleague, still in awe despite the passing years, declared: 'He didn't score ten bloody runs in ten bloody seasons.' For where village cricket is concerned, there are duties more important than hitting a ball with a bat.

In the kingdom of the blind, the one-eyed man is king. Just as surely, in the village cricket field, where water has to be drawn from the well in the far corner, the man who owns the bucket is the boss.

To run a successful team the whole village must be enrolled. Necessarily, the president is a man of substance. But it is no good if his wealth is locked up in stocks and shares, and he is slow to take a hint. He must be able and willing to dig deep and regularly without inquiring too closely as to the need.

A club whose long-serving president had gone to his fathers sighed, partly with sorrow, partly with relief, for while his attention and enthusiasm had been exemplary, he had never fully appreciated the chief implication of his august office.

Seeking a replacement, the committee visited a mill-owner with a country cottage on the village outskirts. Quizzically he listened to their orations and then said, 'They tell me your last president never missed a match and never attended an annual dinner. Well, I shall never attend a match but I shall never miss a dinner', and as this allegorical explanation of his intentions failed to impress, he added, 'I'll never see you go short.'

He filled up their glasses again, and then, amid mutual respects, drove them home in his Rolls.

After the president come the imposing lists of vice-presidents and patrons. The House of Lords may be abolished, Eton and Harrow dismantled (or rejuvenated as propaganda centres for the Tribune group or rest homes for impecunious, disenfranchised MPs) but privilege will never disappear from the village cricket club's list of donors.

All owners of titles, honours and decorations are assiduously cultivated and acknowledged. Colonels and majors become vice-presidents, captains, patrons; baronets, knights and aldermen are made vice-presidents, MPs and councillors merely patrons. Canons and rural deans obviously qualify for the vice-president list, doctors and reverends for the patrons'. Military decorations (except TD) entitle the holder to vice-presidency, but OBEs, MBEs and JPs remain on the patrons' list.

And no-one is merely a mister. Those who can claim no superior or inherited title or impedimenta are styled Esquire. Forlornly, among this roll of male, chauvinistic piggery, is the odd Mrs. Surely, before long, some enterprising secretary will entitle her 'Squiress', and, with pleasure, see her double her subscription.

The most important officer of a local cricket club is the treasurer. Fund-raiser or money-grubber would be a truer, but still an imperfect appellation, for, like a conjuring bucket-shop financier, he has to live on an overdraft, pay out more than is coming in, spend when the kitty is empty, assuage the wrath of his debtors and maintain, throughout, the cheerfulness, bonhomie, aplomb and good humour of one living in a land of milk and honey.

Often the guile of the serpent is required. The treasurer of a church club, congratulated on its apparent affluence, explained, softly and shamefacedly, 'We run a weekly lucky numbers and a pool draw. Just between a few of us. And we keep very quiet about it.' When I remarked what a boon an extension of the scheme might prove, he shook his head sadly. 'No', he sighed, 'we daren't do that. If t'parson got to know he'd stop t'lot.'

The hon. treasurer's business will suffer, his wife threaten divorce, his children's homework will go unchecked, yet through all this adversity and turmoil he must remain smooth, suave, cheerful and carefree. Better than any variety comedian or a Shakespearian tragedian, he knows that the show must go on.

At the annual general meeting the submission of his report will provoke howls of complaints and questions. 'T'joiner tells me', says one club member, 'that you haven't paid him for that wood he let you have to mend t'seats three years since.' 'T'plumber says', grumbles another, 'that he won't mend t'cistern in t'toilet till you've paid his last two bills.' 'How is it', angrily demands a third, 'that there wasn't a new ball for t'second team match when they got into t'semi-final of t'Cup?'

All hands seem to be turned against him till a meek, self-effacing little man stands up. 'My wife tells me', he complains, 'that you refused to buy two new tea towels for t'refreshment tent even though they were selling 'em at half-price in t'Co-op sale. And when she showed you t'ones they'd been using for five years that were full of holes, you laughed in her face and said she'd have to buy 'em out of her own pocket.'

Cheers of admiration ring out for the treasurer's business acumen. He is patted on the back, congratulations pour on him for his shrewdness and care, and, unanimously, he is reappointed.

Besides the president and treasurer, there are innumerable secretaries and committees to deal with fixtures, the refreshment room, subscriptions, ground and playing members. There are umpires to be appointed to the league roster, delegates to attend meetings and conferences arranged at league, area and county level. Village worthies of immaculate character must be appointed to be responsible for the moral welfare of the under-18, under-16 and under-14 teams when they travel away from home on a week-night, or (unless the team has a religious foundation) on a Sunday morning. They have a difficult task, for while they must encourage their young and impressionable charges to emulate their seniors on the cricket field, they must frown sternly on attempts to ape them in their language, their visits to the pub after the match, or the chatting-up of the unattached young dolly birds who flaunt their attractions round the boundary edge.

Let us now forsake these happy mortals and turn to that most misused of all men, the groundsman. I have always felt that bus conducting would be an acceptable occupation if it were not for the passengers. A groundsman must have similar reservations about the players.

He is at the imperious beck and call of everyone. Maurice Leyland once said, on being asked what it felt like to go to bat in a Test Match, 'It's very uncomfortable. You are going to face the best bowler in the world. There are 30,000 people watching you, and they all know better than you how to play him.' A groundsman

Wise in his generation – Ted Wainwright

must feel much the same about the 'experts' advising him, their knowledge of horticulture limited to growing geraniums in a window box.

He must work what are euphemistically called unsocial hours, for in the height of summer he must have the light roller on the wicket before the early morning dew evaporates, and in the evening he must wait until practice has finished before assembling a rolling team to put the heavy one on. His imploring requests meet with a variety of specious excuses; from the married ones that they have to hurry home and baby-sit while their wives go to a chapel concert or to bingo, from the older single ones that they are late for an appointment at the pub, from the youths that they have birds to meet at the disco.

Blithely we talk about the benefits of science, but they have proved a burden to the groundsman unless the team has an ale tent which can provide a mechanical roller from its liquid profits.

When agriculture was a rural craft, a shire horse could be borrowed from the farm, his hooves shod with sacks and, chatting gently to each other – the groundsman chewing straws, the horse sugar lumps – the 'team' could perambulate cheerfully for hours.

Nearly every village club in the West Riding has a story of having purchased a donkey to assist the groundsman with this task. A shed was built for it on the boundary edge but one morning, a month or so later, emaciated and forlorn, it was found slumped in its stable, for although a committee, wise and experienced in husbandry, had been assembled, nobody had been appointed to feed it.

For one club there had seemed a more convenient supply of horses than the farm. 'T'ground', the man responsible told me, 'was next door to t'Leeds and Liverpool Canal, so I used to borrow a barge horse. Now, tha knows, a barge horse isn't like a farm horse. It nobbut has to tug twice to get t'barge moving and then it just walks along t'tow path. Well, this barge horse used to tug twice and when t'roller didn't move it just stood still, and neither braying it nor coaxing it did any good.'

He paused, waiting of course for me to ask, 'What did you do then?'

'Aye, well', he concluded, gratified at my question, 'I used to light a fire under it. When its belly got too warm for its liking it moved off all right.'

Nor is a coach's life all sweetness and light. Particularly if he is at a boarding school, most of his evenings will be spent trying to instil correctitude into youthful arms and wrists, and his little free time will be very welcome.

Ted Wainwright, the old Yorkshire cricketer, had such an appointment when his county career had finished. He had a young net bowler to assist him, and one afternoon, just as they were finishing for the day, a little prep boy came from the school to advise them that one of the masters would like a net that evening.

The youthful net bowler was up in revolt. Perhaps he had an assignation with one of the under-housemaids.

'Tell him it's our night off, Ted', he instructed, angrily. 'Tell him he can't have a net.'

But Ted was no Bolshie. He had been brought up under Lord Hawke's aegis, where intransigence was unthinkable.

'Nay', said Ted, wisely, 'we can't do that. We mun bowl middle and leg with a bit of off spin and hit him in t'goolies as soon as we can.'

UMPIRES

Like the Wise Monkey, the umpire has a duty to 'speak no evil' (or in the case of a Yorkshire monkey, perhaps, to 'hear all, see all and say nowt'). But necessarily, at times, his taciturnity cracks before the antics and vociferousness of those over whom, for a spell, he holds jurisdiction.

A youthful fast bowler, wildly over-enthusiastic, slinging the ball in gay abandon in every direction except straight, yelled an appeal to high heaven every time a ball came in contact with the batsman, be it with his cap neb, navel or batting gloves.

At last the umpire, reluctant as a Trappist abbot berating an erring lay brother, broke his vow of silence: 'What's thy name, lad?'

'Barron,' barked the belligerent bowler. 'What for?'

'Nay, nowt', said the umpire mildly, 'nobbut it's a pity thy mother wasn't.'

Another umpire, in charge of a game where the players' abilities had been minimal, had made decisions irreconcilable with MCC rules. After the match the captain of the losing team approached him. 'By gum', he said forthrightly, 'but thou'rt a lousy umpire.'

'Aye', replied the umpire, unperturbed. 'I know I am. If I'd been any good, do you think they'd have appointed me to umpire a match between two such bloody rotten teams as you are?'

My own first encounter with such an umpire cast us, momentarily, almost to the depths of the Slough of Despond. Young, loud-mouthed insufferably arrogant, we were playing for the Sunday school second team.

In his wisdom, the umpire disagreed with all our stentorian appeals, and when our opponents, with their last men at the wicket, required one run to win, he gave the batsman not out though we had broken the wicket before he was half-way down the pitch.

In the dressing tent, in language that even today would not be tolerated in an XX film, we vented our disgust. When we looked up, alas, there was the errant umpire standing by the uplifted shutter, within sound of every curse and blasphemy we uttered.

Quietly he approached the captain. 'I'd like to speak to one of your chapel deacons', he said. 'Is there one about?' And when we denied all knowledge of their whereabouts he insisted, 'There must be one in t'field somewhere. I'll wait here till you find him.'

Leaden-footed the captain went on his errand, returning at last with the Sunday school worthy.

Most of the players had dressed hurriedly and departed, but a few of us, rooted to the spot, waited for the Sword of Damocles to fall.

As the deacon came in, the umpire put his hand into his trousers pocket, pulled out half a crown and gave it to him. 'There's my match fee for umpiring', he said, 'I never take it when I'm standing for a Sunday school team. Will you put it in t'chapel collection tomorrow?' Briefly he nodded to the deacon, folded up his white coat and departed.

Umpires have changed, much for the worse, since the War. All games and pastimes suffer when they are subject to the deadening hand of science. Cricket has been taken over by the strategists and planners. Performance may advance, but pleasure departs. Games are, primarily, not for winning, they are for enjoying.

The modern umpire, in his white cap, and natty, short, hip-slinky white coat has become a symbol of science. He makes no reply to an appeal and raises his index finger delicately and demurely to give a batsman out, believing it his duty to abase himself almost to a cipher.

It was not so in days of yore. Then the umpire knew he was not a mere adjunct to the game. He was the apex, the great arbiter; he was, on the cricket field, God himself for the duration of a Saturday afternoon. Authoritative and majestic, in a white coat as long as a bridal gown and proud as the bride herself as she walks up the aisle, he strode to the middle.

One season a southern amateur in gaudy cap, had condescended to play in a northern league. After gently stopping the first ball from a slow left-arm bowler with a short run up, he perambulated round the wicket, reassessing the field placings, hitching up his pads and body-guard, twiddling with his gloves.

The bowler, who had started on his run, was held up by the umpire's outstretched arm, until, at last, the batsman had resettled himself to his comfort. Again the batsman poked the ball a yard in front of himself, again he went for his stroll and held his pensive inspection.

But this time, as the bowler moved in there was no restraining hand. Down went the wickets with the batsman in the middle of his investigation. As he heard the smack of the ball against the stumps and saw his wicket tumble, he said, furiously, 'But I wasn't *ready*, umpire.' 'No', answered the umpire gleefully, 'but thou will be t'next time I'm umpiring against thee.'

One of the umpire's duties, in those jolly days, was to be assertive, not to abase himself according to the modern trend. A loud appeal of 'How's that?' would be met with a stentorian roar of 'Not out', and the glare of the aggrieved bowler would be met with an aggressive, searing scowl from the umpire. More than one truculent fast bowler, as the players took the field, has been advised by the umpire, 'It's no good thee bawling thy head off today, lad. I can shout louder than thee.'

It was fun, when we met a new umpire, to establish his decibel rating, so we appealed to high heaven whenever the ball passed with arm's length of a hesitant bat.

We never won. Neither town crier nor RSM could compete with those egotistical arbiters of our Saturday afternoon's fortunes.

Only once do I remember their being defied. We had been fielding for about an hour when a sudden shower sent us scurrying to the pavilion. There is a belief among the innocent that such intervals are used to plan the destruction of the batsman at the wicket. In practice, gloves and pads are swept from the top of a table, a pack of cards is produced with the speed and *élan* of a conjurer, and a game of brag, pontoon or ha'penny nap is soon in full swing.

The shower did not last long. The umpires walked sedately to the middle and waved for us to follow them. There was no response. Fully fifteen minutes had gone before we emerged and the game was resumed. There were headlines in the paper, 'Team refuses to take field. Complains pitch too wet'. And when we were reported to the League executive, our secretary, pleading with all the skill of a QC and pointing out the danger of greasy run-ups to fast bowlers, the seriousness of torn ligaments, pulled muscles and damaged hamstrings, sighed with relief when we escaped with a severe admonition as to future conduct.

Not even a whisper emerged that no self-respecting cricket team would leave the dressing tent to continue the game until a pontoon kitty of over £1 had been won by someone.

But more duties than the interpretation of the MCC rules fall to the lot of the village umpire. They are at the beck and call of everyone, armed with dictatorial powers but requiring the wisdom of a white-coated Solomon.

In a village match a slow bowler stationed a fieldsman suicidally close at very forward short leg. The bowler, alas, had not the accuracy of Ray Illingworth or Hedley Verity. Soon he dropped one short. Gleefully the batsman swung round and caught the ball on the meat of the bat.

Straight against the fieldsman's shin it cracked. There was a spurt of blood, a howl of pain. Immediately, the fallen warrior was surrounded by umpires, colleagues, bowler, fieldsmen and wicket-keeper, while out from the pavilion galloped the first-aid man.

What was happening inside that tight, white circle we could not see, but soon an anxious umpire trotted out to a spectator.

'T'first aid man wants to borrow thy penknife', said the umpire to the spectator. 'He's bahn to cut it off.'

The spectator looked at him in astonishment. 'Hasn't he sent for a doctor or t'ambulance?' he asked in disbelief.

'No', said the umpire.

'Well', said the spectator, in a fine display of humanity, 'he can't go cutting a man's leg off without getting a doctor's permission.'

'It's nooan his leg he's bahn to cut off', said the umpire, 'it's t'end of t'bandage. He wants to borrow thy knife because he's forgotten his scissors.'

MORE UMPIRES

Trueman 'bowled at upwards of 90 mph'.

It is strange that, usually, we employ old men to umpire. Scientists (with what justification they never say) tell us that 'Typhoon' Tyson, Harold Larwood, Fred Trueman and such-like hurtlers bowled at upwards of 90 mph.

We may assume, therefore, again with no justification whatsoever, that our village demon can attain 60. Without calling in a senior wrangler or borrowing computers, log. tables or pocket calculators, we can therefore calculate the time the ball takes to cross the wicket as $(60 \times 22 \times 60) \div (1760 \times 60)$ seconds, which, unless you have forgotten your school work on fractions, vulgar and improper, works out at $3/4$ of a second.

The umpire, myopic, hypermetropic, astigmatic or suffering from atrophy of the accommodation muscles, is expected, in $3/4$ of a second, to watch the ball cross the wicket, swerve in the air, swing off the pitch, deviate from off or from leg, at the same time noticing if the bowler has overstepped the popping crease.

A fast bowler once swung the ball full toss on to the batsman's pad. At his appeal the ancient umpire raised his finger. 'I never saw that ball', complained the batsman. 'No', agreed the umpire cheerfully, 'neither did I.'

The surprise is that they *ever* see them. Perhaps they never do. And if we were certain that were true, what a wonderful boon it would be for cricket. No more would the batsman need to play defensively or watch, apprehensively, as the ball, pitching outside his off stump, whipped through to the wicket-keeper. He could drive at the ball with gay abandon, cut and leg glance with glorious impunity, hook with unmitigated exuberance. For whether he snicked the ball or not would depend not on actuality but on the whim of the umpire. Tediousness and lack-lustre play would be abolished. Nihilism, for the duration of an innings, would triumph.

To see umpires in all their pristine glory you should visit their Winter Olympics. You will not find the location easy to discover, and even if you find it, entry will probably be refused.

Like members of a forbidden society they assemble secretly; the four star men from each of several leagues being chosen to join in dauntless combat, with quarter neither asked for nor given.

A bench of judges is empanelled. Roneod sheets are distributed to the competitors, containing purple diagrams of wickets, bats and padded legs, with dotted lines showing the paths and vagaries of hallucinatory balls; and on these sheets the umpires, in their wisdom, must give decisions on such debatable points as leg before wicket, run out, obstructing the field, no balls and stumped.

They then depart to an outer room and each in turn, like witnesses at a murder trial, is brought forth to answer awkward questions.

'Describe the pitch', a judge ordered one.

'Ah', said the pride of his league, 'there are three wickets at each end, and', attempting to gild the lily and win a bonus point and the plaudits of his committee, 'the middle one shall be in the centre.'

Another question was, 'The ball strikes your colleague in the middle of the forehead and knocks him unconscious. What should you do?'

'Ho-ho', laughed the man next to me joyfully, a league secretary, 'our chap's a porter at Victoria Hospital. Wait till he comes in.'

The porter duly arrived and was presented with the conundrum. He, in his phantasy, returned to the pavilion and fetched the first aid kit which he always carried. He sent for the doctor, the ambulance, the fire brigade and the police and put the coroner on stand-by.

The correct answer was simply, 'Immediately call Dead Ball.'

In the golden days before instant cricket and limited overs raised their ugly heads, cup ties started on a Monday evening, continued on a Tuesday evening, a Wednesday evening, a Thursday evening, a Friday evening, a Monday evening... ad infinitum; the only concession to eternity being that innings were suspended at 150 runs.

We had batted on the Monday evening in a vital cup-tie and suspended at 150 for 4 wickets, and on the Tuesday evening our opponents had replied with 150 runs for 5 wickets. Now the obstacle to this delightful illimitability was that umpires were paid for two nights only. Thereafter they received only expenses.

On the Wednesday night we continued our batting to about 270 all out, and our opponents took up their suspended innings. Dusk fell, a damp mist rose from the river, the street lights were lit, the last bus had gone.

At last the batsman spoke to the umpires about the dwindling light, but they, after a long consultation, decided to carry on.

As I was about to deliver the next ball the batsman held up his hand and asked politely for the sight board to be moved.

It seemed a strange request as I had not changed the angle of my bowling and all had seemed satisfactory for the last hour.

'Yes', I said, 'do you want it moving right or left?'

'Neither', snapped the angry batsman. 'I want it bringing nearer. I can't see the bloody thing.'

My two favourite umpires were separated by aeons of time; the first I met when I was a schoolboy, the second when spectators had long been saying, 'How much longer is that old bugger bahn to go on laiking?'

We were playing a school match away against a Manchester grammar school. It was in the days when Yorkshire's batting array began *Holmes, Sutcliffe, Oldroyd, Leyland,* and Lancashire's *Hallows, Makepeace, Ernest Tyldesley,* but there was as much Roses flavour in our match as in the duels at Old Trafford and Headingley.

It was a day-long match, and each side provided its own umpire – they, their august, learned and enthusiastic headmaster; we, a sixth-form crony.

We batted first on a fast and fiery wicket. Our opening batsman quickly retired for stitching and possibly cosmetic surgery, and soon I was standing wary at the wicket. Well knowing discretion to be the better part of valour, I took up a stance near the square leg umpire, holding out a horizontal bat. In my first over, three vociferous appeals for caught behind the wicket were turned down.

At last, thankfully, I reached the other end. 'Harry', said my umpire crony anxiously, 'if thou snicks any more I shall have to give thee out.'

The day had a happy ending. We were bowled out for 39 long before lunch. We were defending an unbeaten record, and when their enthusiastic headmaster suggested making it a double innings match, we readily concurred, feeling that perhaps we could make a draw of it and save our bacon.

But before lunch we had bowled out the Manchester school for 32, changed our minds about a second innings, claimed victory and dashed off to Blackpool to spend the afternoon and evening in the Tower Ballroom with the delectable Lancashire dolly birds.

On the second occasion I was batting with an exuberant, youthful colleague unable to understand the ravages that time had wrought on my acceleration.

He played the ball to short mid-wicket and called me for an impossible run.

Scrambling across a pitch that looked as wide and unfriendly as the Sahara Desert, I was at least a foot short of the popping crease when the bails were whipped off. Involuntarily I looked to square leg and there was the umpire, finger upraised, running towards the wicket. And then, unbelievably, he dropped his finger and said, 'Just in'.

Umpires, long and short and tall; bless 'em all.

MARRIAGE GUIDANCE

Billy Bates played for Yorkshire in the 1880s. Unlike his rustic team mates, he was so immaculate that he was christened 'The Duke'. Billy had a soft spot for ladies. In 1881 he went with Shaw and Shrewsbury's team to Australia. When they rested at the Sandwich Islands, now known as Hawaii, the local monarch (probably a cannibal) came on board ship every day to hear Billy sing 'The Bonny Yorkshire Lass'.

When Billy was so thoughtless as to get married in the middle of a cricket season, his crony Ted Peate exclaimed in disgust, 'Bates is a fool. He's gone and got wed in t'middle of summer. He ought to have waited till t'middle of winter when he could give his undivided attention to it.'

Years later, another famous county cricketer, married to a jealous wife, was picked to tour Australia. This was in the days before space travel had shrunk the world, and Australia was still a six-week's ocean journey away.

Before he set sail, his wife treated him to a tirade of explicit instructions about behaving himself, avoiding loose company, not trying to match the Aussies pint for pint, keeping out of low dives, and above all, not taking up with any of those fast hussies who, she had heard, made themselves available to sporting celebrities.

Furthermore, she demanded that he write home regularly.

But when they arrived in Australia there was all the novelty of a new country, there was acclimatisation, the net practices to attend, the physical preparations to be undertaken, the early State matches to play, success in which decided the Test Team.

Not until two months after he had left home did he find time for correspondence, and even then he could only spare a minute to scribble off a cablegram which was meant to read, 'Having wonderful time. Wish you were here.'

Alas, the decipherer of his message left off the last letter e. And what his agonised and suspicious wife read, when it was delivered, was 'Wish you were her'.

Any young lady who marries a cricketer condemns herself to a life of neglect and slavery. She will be expected to wait at home on a Saturday evening, putting the children to bed and bathing the baby while her lord and master whiles away a couple of hours with his team mates in the pub, replaying the lost game. He will bring home a pair of flannels, viridescent down one leg where he has fallen missing a catch, pillar box red down the other, where he has tried to retain the shine on the ball, and expect them to be white as driven snow for the cup tie on Monday evening.

He will expect her to bake buns, biscuits and cakes, serve and wash up in the tea tent. In winter there will be pies and stews to make for fund-raising pie suppers; there will be coffee mornings, bring and buy sales, good-as-new and white elephant stalls to organise; jars of home-made chutney, blackberry jam and orange marmalade to be boiled, bottles of dandelion, rhubarb and cowslip wine to be fermented and slabs of home-made toffee to be rolled and broken for the annual Autumn Fayre.

But until he has got the ring on her finger and has imprisoned her in his gilded cage, the young innocent will know nothing of this toil and labour.

He will sit with her at the boundary edge adopting an heroic posture, recounting, with appropriate gestures, stirring tales of derring-do, explaining how he won the cup final by hitting the last ball of the match out of the field for a six; of how he could be opening Yorkshire's innings with Geoff Boycott had he not declined the offer for love of her. When he is bowled out for a duck, first ball, he will have the effrontery to come back to her and say, 'I could have hit that ball for a four. I could have scored fifty and won the match, but I knew you wanted to get away early to go dancing, love, so I let them bowl me out.'

He will leave her, 'just for a minute, sweetheart', hurry to the pavilion, pack his bag and throw it to his mother in the tea tent, 'I'll want 'em clean and pressed for the five-a-side match I'm playing in tomorrow afternoon', he'll say. Then, with his bird on his arm, he will saunter out of the field before the match is finished on his way to Annabelle's Disco or the Pretty Polly night club . . . to the undying disgust of his captain.

Gently, insidiously, he will lead her up the garden path to a life of sweat and toil, for while no man should play football after he is 30 or bowls before he is 50, there are no such age limits for cricketers. Wilfred Rhodes played for Yorkshire until he was 52; George Hirst turned out in a Festival Match at Scarborough when he was 59; Lord Hawke was still captain of Yorkshire when he was 50; Joe Rowbotham was 52 when he retired in 1883; Herbert Sutcliffe played in a match when he was 50; David Hunter stumped till he was 49, and Emmott Robinson began a long county career when he was 35.

Not until years after critical spectators have been asking, 'How much longer is that old devil going to be laiking?' will our heroine's husband contemplate retirement. From 15 to 50 he will have played every Saturday, some Sundays and many evenings. They will have missed the first Saturday of their annual holidays and come back early on the second so that he could play in the derby match against the Primitive Methodists or the Wesleyan Reform.

Even on their holidays there will have been times when he has left her on the sands at Blackpool to build sand castles and buy candy floss for their quiverful of children, while he came back home to play in a Sunday school league cup tie.

Even in his middle fifties, when the selection committee sighs in relief as he suggests, 'Happen I'll stand down next season and make way for one of t'youngsters', this does not mean he has finished.

For the next fifteen years his flannels have to be immaculately washed and pressed, his shirt ironed, his bat oiled, his boots whitened, and his cap brushed. Every Saturday, enviously, hopefully, he will lug his bag up to the cricket field, and if the second team is a man short, he will speedily strip and joyfully take the field.

He will drop catches, he will misfield, he will stumble over the boundary rope, he will run men out through his irresolution and lack of nimbleness between the wickets.

Inevitably, he will lose the match for them, and, for a week afterwards, will hobble about with a stick as lumbago and sciatica bend him agonisingly double.

Nevertheless, on the Saturday following, there he is again. 'They tell me Jimmy Baldwin's wife is expecting again today', he will say, and add, hopefully, 'I don't see how you can expect him to play. Do you think I'd better get changed?'

But by the time he has undressed to vest and underpants Jimmy will come bustling into the tent. Timidly, they will mention his wife's condition. 'Oh', he will say airily, 'I've left her with my grandmother and her Aunt Minnie. It isn't her first, tha knows. I expect they'll know what to do. And if they don't, I can't help 'em.'

By the time he is 45 our hero will have his eldest son in the second team, another in the under-18s and a third in the juniors. The child is father of the man; like chips off the old block, they will also have bags of sweaty cricket shirts and flannels to wash, till the clothes line in the family garden resembles the Mall on Jubilee Day.

It is the time, now, that both the woe-begone wife and the cricket club consider the eldest son ready for marriage.

Contemplatively, the elders of the chapel consider the maidens of their own religious persuasion and divide them into three groups, the pretty, the passable and the unlovely. The last they will ignore.

The first group, those with sylph-like figures, alluring countenances and provocative glances they will despatch, like Joshua and Caleb to the Promised Land, to the socials and dances held by the Methodists and the Unitarians to capture some impressionable youth who is also a star cricketer and bring him into their fold, for it is well known that the youth will follow his heart-throb back to her place of worship and join their cricket club.

The middle group are paired off with their own local lads, but although our hero's first-born was thrown together with the maiden chosen for him, little progress towards their nuptials was made. He seemed to be drifting to lifelong bachelorhood, with his mother's washload never to be lifted.

Then one evening their daughter, a young lady with measurements fit to grace Miss World, who had been despatched on her mission to the Anglicans, came bursting into the living room.

'Mother', she said, all smiles, 'I've started courting Willie Priestley of St. Oswald's. Him that goes in first for them, and he's going to come and laik for us next season.'

'Ee', said her mother, 'thy dad will be suited.'

'Aye', said the lass, 'but there's nobbut one thing. He hasn't a mother, so I said he could bring his cricket clothes back here after t'match. I knew you wouldn't mind washing 'em along with all ours. . . .'

All of which reminds me of the sorry tale of Seth Ackroyd. . . .

THE KNIGHT THAT MIGHT HAVE BEEN

In the early 1920s, Seth Ackroyd, then in his late teens, was regarded by his village locals as the greatest cricketing prospect Yorkshire had ever known. It was confidently predicted that in a couple of years' time, when Seth had reached maturity, Yorkshire would be able to dispense with the services of both Herbert Sutcliffe and Wilfred Rhodes.

But one Wakes Saturday, Seth, like all the rest of the mobile inhabitants of the village, transported himself to Blackpool, and being, like Dr. W. G. Grace, a famous dancer, went immediately to the Tower Ballroom to see what female talent Lancashire could provide to entertain him during his holidays.

Seth picked her up in the first valeta. She was a honey, with smooth, silky jet black hair with a snow white beret perched saucily on top, a black and white polka-dot frock and long, shapely Charleston legs. Rapturously they gazed into each other's eyes and saw the lovelight.

Coffee mornings, afternoon tea dances and evening assemblies saw them demonstrate their immaculate skills at the foxtrot, quickstep, tango, military two step and destiny waltz. Between dancing sessions they strolled, arms entwined, lost in their contemplation of each other, along the promenade and the Golden Mile.

The rest of the village, between paddling, gobbling Blue Point oysters and supping bottled ale, watched them unperturbed.

It would be no bad thing, they opined, for Seth to learn at first hand of the cunning, duplicity, deceitfulness and trickery of Lancashire females, and when he had worked her out of his system he could settle down with some homely village lass who would cook him three meals a day and addle a bit of brass in the mill as a burler and mender or a twister.

On the last day of the holidays she turned up to wave him goodbye and, as the train steamed out of the station, there were fond embraces, tearful and heartrending kisses.

Quickly the village tried to settle down to normality. On Sunday the parson, having been apprised of this crisis in Seth's affairs, preached from Chapter Two of St. Paul's Epistle to the Colossians – *Beware lest any man spoil you through philosophy and vain deceit,* substituting *woman* for *man* and, launching a powerful diatribe against every human being west of the Pennine Chain.

On the Friday evening following, Seth wandered up to the cricket field. 'Will you cross my name off the team for tomorrow?' he asked sheepishly. Immediately there was consternation. Questions were asked about his health, and preparations made for dispatching a little lad to fetch the doctor. 'Nay', said Seth, when at last he could get a word in, 'I aren't poorly. But I'm going to Rochdale tomorn to see Mirabelle.'

From tap room, chapel council meeting and bed the cricket committee was summoned, but neither fulmination nor pleading could divert Seth from his reprobate's path. Every Saturday morning to the end of the season Seth was to be seen catching the early morning train for Manchester Victoria.

This nonsense of Mirabelle's witchery continued into the winter. One evening Isaiah Haigh, chairman of the cricket club and chapel worthy, and his wife were discussing the impasse.

'I've been wondering', said Mrs. Haigh, 'if anybody in t'village could put this Mirabelle up for t'weekends next summer, or 'appen – although Seth's nobbut nineteen – they could get wed and live over here.'

'Aye', mused Isaiah, 'thou's taken t'words right out of my mouth. I were nobbut thinking if he happened to put her in t'family way. . . .'

'Isaiah!' shrieked Mrs. Haigh, 'an' thee a chapel deacon! I'm downright ashamed of thee. No such thought had ever entered my head.'

Nevertheless, the germ of an idea had been planted. By spring the wedding was arranged for the Saturday before the season started and the village had clubbed up to buy them a little cottage near Chapel Fold, while many families interested in the cricket club had provided a minimum of second-hand furniture.

All was set for the opening match, but, alas, at five minutes to three there was no sign of Seth. A deputation was sent to hurry him along, but when they knocked on the door of the cottage, it was opened by Mirabelle, a veritable virago of anger.

'Cricket!' she stormed at them. 'I'm not interested in your silly games. Seth's painting the kitchen and whitewashing the cellar'. And to another inquiry she snapped, 'No, you *can't* have a word with him. I've told him he can't play and that's the end of it', and she banged the door in their faces.

Tragically, without Seth's aid, the team drifted to the bottom of the league, but, a month into the season, on the Monday of the first round of the cup, Mirabelle was seen, by the eye of every gossip in the village, to be setting off on her weekly jaunt to Lancashire to visit her mother. And it was known that she always came back on the nine o'clock train.

At six o'clock in the evening the club committee were knocking on the door of cottage. 'Nay', said the shamefaced Seth, draped in his woolsorter's apron, 'I daren't laik tonight. Mirabelle's telled me to paper t'back bedroom. She'll make my life a misery if it isn't finished by t'time she gets back tonight.'

'Ee', chortled the committee, in relief and delight, 'don't thee fret thisen. We'll paper t'back bedroom. Get thee off up to t'cricket field.'

It was 8.30. Dusk was settling. The visitors had batted first and scored 95. Amid the shambles of the home team's reply, Seth stood firm. He was 48 not out, and the score was 92 for 9 wickets.

Suddenly a commotion was seen at the distant gate. Mirabelle had come back on an earlier train! A termagant of hatred and determination, she dashed on to the pitch, raised her umbrella and belaboured Seth across the shoulders until it snapped under her fury. Then, seizing him by the hair, she dragged him from the field and across Chapel Fold to the cottage.

'Well', said the imperturbable umpire, ten minutes later, 'I don't think yond'll come back tonight. I'm sorry, but you've lost.'

In the morning the cottage was empty and deserted. No more was ever seen or heard of Seth and Mirabelle.

There were rumours, from time to time, from those foolish enough to travel into Lancashire, that Seth had been spotted, in Bury, in Bolton, in Haslingden, in Accrington, in Bacup . . . and always it was hinted that he was painting a kitchen, glazing a greenhouse, creosoting a hut, fixing a clothes prop, donkey-stoning a doorstep, sweeping a chimney or crazy-paving a garden path . . .

And so Len Hutton arose, became the greatest batsman in the world, took England to Australia, won the Ashes and, for his services to cricket, was dubbed Sir Leonard.

So easily – had it not been for Mirabelle – it could have been Sir Seth. . . .

SACKCLOTH

The County Cricket Championship was instituted in 1877, Gloucestershire being the winners with eight victories in nine matches. In 1878 Middlesex played six matches, won three and drew three and claimed top position.

Yorkshire's first success came in 1893. They won again in 1896 and 1898, and then, in the 36 playing seasons from 1900 to 1939, were champions 18 times, besides being placed second in 1904, 1906, 1907, 1913, 1926 and 1929.

In 1900 they won 16 matches and lost none; in 1901 they won 20 and lost 1; in 1902, won 13, lost 1; in 1908, won 16, lost none; in 1912, won 13, lost 1; in 1923, won 25, lost 1; in 1925, won 21, lost none; in 1931, won 16, lost 1; in 1935, won 19 lost 1.

In 1926, when they were second, they did not lose a match, nor did they in 1928, when they were fourth.

In those 36 seasons they won 543 matches and lost 93. In their separate eras the cricket grounds of England were bestrode by Yorkshire's George Hirst, Wilfred Rhodes, Schofie Haigh, Stanley Jackson, David Denton, Herbert Sutcliffe, Maurice Leyland, Roy Kilner, George Macaulay, Len Hutton, Hedley Verity and Bill Bowes.

Defeats averaged less than three a season and often the Yorkshire team was decimated by Test Match and Gentlemen v Players calls, for besides those mentioned, Percy Holmes, Wilf Barber, Major Booth, Arthur Wood and Arthur Mitchell played for England.

George Hirst, in his coaching days, at Park Avenue.

Wilfred (no surname required) in famous action.

But never were they beset by injury. Before the modern epoch discovered hamstrings, tendons and discs, and medical science invented physiotherapists to work on them, cricketers were never injured.

So, without delving too deeply, lest we turn up long hidden truths that might discredit a pleasant theory, we may put down Yorkshire's rare defeats to the call of Test matches, occasional aberrations and, perhaps, an understandable desire to make the County Championship more competitive and entertaining when, by midseason Yorkshire's lead was overlong.

Nevertheless, five times Yorkshire were ground into the dust. So let us now abase ourselves, don sackcloth and rub our skulls with ashes; let us do what Yorkshiremen have never done before since the second day, when the firmament divided the waters from the waters; let us humble ourselves!

Not particularly auspicious for Yorkshire was the season of 1892. There were men playing for the county that posterity has not honoured: T. Wardall, J. Mounsey, Mr. R. W. Frank, Mr. F. E. Woodhead, H. Hayley. They won five matches and lost five, and in that delightfully simplistic system of scoring that was favoured at the time (and which might, with benefit, be reintroduced today) finished up with no points. No men, you might think, ever strove so long for so little, but you would be mistaken. Gloucestershire won one match and lost eight, and accumulated (although that can hardly be the right word) minus 7 points.

Against Leicestershire at Bradford, in early July, Yorkshire scored 509 runs, declared; Bobby Peel making 226 not out and Ted Wainwright 122, but later in the month, at Leeds, they had been dismissed abysmally by Middlesex for 46. The innings started with Lord Hawke, 0, Louis Hall, 0, to be followed, at number four, by George Ulyett, also 0.

Still, they had Somerset to play twice, and as Somerset had only just been promoted to first-class status and could only muster three professionals among their list of 18 players, two victories appeared certain.

They met first on Thursday and Friday, August 11 and 12 at Sheffield. Like a reaper in the harvest field, Stanley Jackson demolished Somerset. Seventy four was all they made with only one man reaching double figures, but Yorkshire started depressingly (George Ulyett, 0; Lord Hawke, again 0) and scored only 110.

Somerset replied with 248. The task of scoring 213 proved far beyond Yorkshire's resources: they were out for 125, the game finishing on the Friday afternoon.

Now, we must always look for excuses for Yorkshire's failures, however weak (or, lame, as a Yorkshireman would say) they might be.

Matches in those days were played on a Thursday, Friday and Saturday; Saturday being the last day and not, as now, the first. If a match could be finished by Friday, then many of the Yorkshire professionals would have lucrative Saturday afternoon appointments with town and village clubs. Dare we impugn that George Ulyett, Ted Wainwright, John Tunnicliffe, Bobby Peel and J. T. Brown had other pressing engagements on their minds besides the conquest of Somerset? Or shall we leave it with *Wisden* that 'on a fiery wicket they never looked like making the requisite runs'.

A fortnight later the return fixture was at Taunton, and here was the chance to show the cider apple boys how to play cricket.

Yorkshire batted first, scored a commendable 299 and looked forward to rubbing the upstarts' noses in the dust.

Mr. Palairet and Mr. Hewett began the Somerset reply and batted and batted... and batted. 'Somerset', said a report, 'have done many things to render themselves famous in the cricket world. Among all their achievements, however, nothing has been more extraordinary nor has caused such a vast amount of excitement as what was done in this match against Yorkshire.'

At the end of the day's play they were 78 for no wicket. At lunch on the second day they were 301 for no wicket. 'This', went on the report, 'being the first time in an important match that 300 had been put on the board without a wicket down, a special photograph was taken of the figure.'

It was 346 before Hewett was bowled by Peel for 201. Palairet made 146 and W. C. Hedley, coming in at number four, rattled up another 102.

The last wicket fell at 592 just before close of play on the Friday evening.

Nothing but ignoble defeat faced Yorkshire on the Saturday, but when daylight came, rain was falling and it continued throughout the day, 'There never seemed much prospect of cricket, but the captains were so reluctant to give up the idea of

Peel – on a less than fiery wicket?

finishing the match that it was not until half-past four in the afternoon that it was agreed to abandon the contest as a draw', concluded the report.

We can understand Mr. Hewett's laudable desire to rub Yorkshire's nose in the mud. He was no lover of Yorkshire and in 1895, when he was chosen to captain England against Yorkshire at the Scarborough festival, he withdrew from the match because of the 'horseplay of the spectators' who 'vented their displeasure on him' because he considered the wicket unfit for play after bad weather.

But Lord Hawke? His Lordship would be packing his bag and ordering a cabby to drive him to the station at the first drop of rain, rather than see Yorkshire slither to an innings defeat.

Why the aberration? Why the meek surrender to the will of the opposing captain in his desire to humiliate his Yorkshire enemies?

The answer is simple: Lord Hawke was not playing that day. Ernest Smith was the captain.

It was 1901. Yorkshire, champion county in 1900 without the loss of a match, were still undefeated. Again they were playing Somerset, at Leeds on Monday, Tuesday and Wednesday, July 15, 16 and 17.

Somerset batted first. Mr. Palairet got 0, Len Braund 0, V. T. Hill 0, E. Robson 0, A. E. Newton 0. In no time they were all out for 87, Wilfred Rhodes taking 5 wickets for 39 runs.

Yorkshire, the champions, unbeaten for nearly two years, hammered their impotent foes all over Headingley. By close of play on the Monday they had scored 325, Schofield Haigh making 96, George Hirst 61, Wilfred Rhodes 44.

Bewildered Somerset, 238 behind, booked out of their hotels and ordered their carriages for mid-afternoon on Tuesday.

But the spirit of 1892 descended on Mr. Palairet, scion of a great sporting family. Not for nothing was his father for many years England's champion archer! Palairet had already that season scored 100 against Yorkshire at Taunton. Going in first, as usual, this time with Len Braund, he scored 178 in less than four hours. Braund got 107, F. A. Philips hit 122, Sammy Woods scored 66, Vernon Hill 53, and Robson 40.

By close of play they were 549 for 5 wickets. Lord Hawke gaped with amazement at the holocaust. 'I am not captious or grudging', he whined, 'but we all knew Braund was caught at slip by the fairest of catches before the hundred was up. After that, I never seemed to get my boys going again.'

The 238 first innings deficit had been turned into a lead of over 300. Sammy Woods, the Somerset captain, Antipodean-born, a famous Rugby forward, doubtless with the memory of many previous humiliations in mind, licked his lips in anticipation on the Wednesday morning. The vaunted enemy were at his mercy. The wicket was crumbling.

Deliberately and cruelly he ordered the heaviest roller in Headingley to be put on for the full time allowed, breaking up the wicket completely.

Again Lord Hawke showed his pique. 'I remember telling him', he complained, 'I really thought he was a better sportsman, for he well knew that we never had an earthly of getting the runs.'

But Sammy was taking no chances. Wilfred Rhodes polished off Somerset for 630 on the Wednesday morning. Except for Wilfred's, the bowling averages were disastrous; George Hirst, 1 wicket for 189 runs; Ted Wainwright 1 for 107, J. T. Brown 1 for 92.

No roller could improve the wicket now. Ingloriously Yorkshire were all out for 113, losing by 279 runs. 'To the wonderful victory gained by Somerset, cricket history can furnish few parallels', lauded one report.

Somerset finished the season with 4 wins and 10 defeats; Yorkshire did not lose another match, winning the championship with a percentage of 90.47 Middlesex were second with 50.00, Lancashire third with 37.50.

Again, in the delightful and honest scoring system of those days, Somerset finished with minus 42.85, a little better than bottom club Derbyshire, who, incongruously, ended with minus 100 per cent.

... AND ASHES

Let us now, in all humility, turn to Whitsuntide, 1924, to Saturday, Monday and Tuesday, June 7, 9 and 10 the Roses Match at Headingley.

Saturday was a dull day, rain interrupting play. Lancashire batted with all the caution of the fearful, letting George Macaulay bowl 33 overs for 40 runs and Roy Kilner 26 for 28 runs. They only scored 113, but it took Yorkshire 90 overs and almost the whole of the day to get them out. Monday was a good day, both for the weather and for Yorkshire. Although they only headed the enemy's score by 17, Kilner and Macaulay bowled Lancashire out in their second innings for 74.

And so on to Whit Tuesday, June 10, 1924, a beautiful late spring day. Yorkshire needed only 57 runs to beat the Red Rose foe. It was the day that was meant to be the happiest in my life.

It was the day of our annual Congregational Sunday school Whitsuntide Walk. We would march up and down the village with our harmonium, intersecting the Anglicans and the Wesleyans, sing 'Jesus shall reign where'er the sun', 'At the name of Jesus every knee shall bow', 'Love divine, all loves excelling', 'Oft in danger, oft in woe', and 'Through the night of doubt and sorrow', under the windows of the aged and the bedridden. There would follow a bun fight with scalding hot tea from burnished, copper urns in some cow pasture and then, in the evening, there would be dancing in the field, and I had an assignation with a gorgeous Methody bird.

But, as we assembled in the Sunday school with our cups and spoons, each with coloured thread round it for identification, first the rumour, then the fact ran like wildfire round the room. Dick Tyldesley and Cecil Parkin, in just over an hour, had bowled out Yorkshire for 33. Percy Holmes had got a duck; so had Maurice Leyland. Herbert Sutcliffe and Edgar Oldroyd had each scored 3, Emmott Robinson 2.

Forlornly, that evening, I went to meet the Methody bird, and found her smiling and dancing with one of the red-uniformed bandsmen who had been playing in the afternoon for the toffee-nosed Anglicans. I put my hand on her shoulder, but she ignored me and looked lovingly into her partner's eyes. Indubitably, in modern parlance, I had been given the elbow.

'The White Ship' may have been written on the heart of King Henry I. It was etched no deeper than Whit Tuesday, June 10, 1924, is on mine.

There was another unfortunate match in 1924. Yorkshire had won the County Championship and as was usual in those distant days, played The Rest of England at the Oval, at the end of the season. 'It had been intended to revert to the old custom of giving four days to the annual match at the Oval between the Champion County and The Rest of England, but last September it was cut down to three', said *Wisden*.

An unhappy incident concerning another county may have caused the shortening of the play. The county, which we will not name, had won the championship and four days had been allocated to the match. That county's opening batsman, a senior player, went to see his committee and inquired how much they were to be paid. The same, he was told, as for a county match. 'But', he

George Macaulay (better known as a bowler).

complained, 'this is a four-day match. County matches only last three days.' But he was given no comfort and therefore proposed to his team-mates that they should make sure the game lasted only three days.

With this in mind, he quickly allowed himself to be dismissed on the first morning. Alas, his team-mates refused to follow his truculent example, and made a huge score to which The Rest of England responded with one correspondingly large.

'Very well', said the senior player, in high dudgeon on the morning of the last day, 'if it's a four-day match you want I may as well bat the whole of the last day.' Which he did, gently, unhurriedly, ignoring the prospects of either victory or defeat, but with all the artistry and consummate skill of which he was capable.

So shall we excuse Yorkshire, and say they went into The Rest of England match with little interest or ambition?

Batting first on a beautiful wicket Yorkshire scored only 166, and by the end of the day The Rest were 165 for two wickets. On the second day, the Yorkshire bowling was mercilessly punished.

Frank Woolley scored 202, Percy Chapman 74, his last 60 coming in 25 minutes. Three overs yielded 49 runs; 21 and 10 off Wilfred Rhodes, 18 off Abe Waddington, and poor Wilfred finished with no wickets for 124 runs. 'In cheerless weather the match ended tamely', said a report. Yorkshire, in their second innings, scored 234 in reply to The Rest's 524 for 8 wickets declared. They lost by an innings and 124 runs.

Had they really had a surfeit of cricket by mid-September, having played 30 county matches besides games against Cambridge University, the South Africans, MCC, Scotland and Forfarshire? Were even those great competitors, Herbert Sutcliffe, Roy Kilner, Percy Holmes and Wilfred himself, sick to death at the sight of a cricket field?

It was 1935, Wednesday and Thursday, July 31 and August 1, at Huddersfield, 'the match that produced the sensation of the season'. Yorkshire, three-quarters of the way through the season, were playing Essex.

Cheerfully, on winning the toss, they went in first. Before half-past twelve they were all out for 31, H. D. Read taking six wickets for 11 runs, Maurice Nichols 4 for 17. When two early wickets had fallen Maurice Leyland laughed, 'I can play these with a walking stick.' His two innings resulted in: Bowled Read 0 . . . and bowled Read 2.

It was Yorkshire's lowest score for 26 years. There was no reason or excuse for it. Essex went in, played Bowes and Verity with little trouble, and scored 334.

Yorkshire followed on. Again the two demolishers of their first innings wrought their evil will. In their second innings 99 was all that Yorkshire could muster. Young and old alike withered before the menace. Individual scores read:

H. Sutcliffe, c. Sheffield, b. Nichols	4	c. Eastman, b. Nichols	1
A B. Sellers, c. Wilcox, b. Read	2	L.B.W., b. Nichols	2
L. Hutton, b. Nichols	0	L.B.W., b. Nichols	0

The two Yorkshire innings lasted less than three hours. There was no reason for it; no extenuation of it. It was the only county match they lost all season. They came straight to Bradford, bowled Lancashire out for 53 and won by seven wickets. At the end of the season, for the first time for 30 years, as Champion County they beat The Rest of England by 149 runs, and Read, the evil demon of their Huddersfield debacle, had to be satisfied with 3 wickets for 122 runs.

But while deploring Yorkshire's feeble display, we must pay honour to Maurice Nichols, the Essex all-rounder, who produced what was probably the finest individual performance of all time in county cricket. Yorkshire, in their two innings scored 130 runs. Nichols, in his one innings, scored 146, and, in the match took 11 wickets for 54 runs.

Tom Hunt, the single wicket champion, in 1845 beat Eleven of Knaresborough. Truthfully it can be said that in 1935 Nichols, alone, beat the cream of Yorkshire.

But after the rain comes the sun, after night, day, after the last post, reveille.

In 1937 Yorkshire, as usual, won the championship, but they only just pipped Middlesex at the post, and at Lord's, in the middle of June, Middlesex had beaten Yorkshire by an innings. Both in batting and bowling Yorkshire had failed dismally. Sutcliffe had got a duck in his second innings, Mitchell scored 1 and 3; Leyland 1 and 19; Hutton 7 and 19. It was a sorry display, for Middlesex made over 400, only two of their batsmen failing to reach double figures.

The return match at Sheffield was rained off, but again Yorkshire were the underdogs. They had lost on the first innings, and only Hutton was defying the Londoners in the second when rain came.

Ruefully the Middlesex team surveyed their frustrating season, and reflected on their ill luck. They were, in their own opinion, a much better team than Yorkshire. The evil jinx that had visited them must be exorcised. Champions, statistically, Yorkshire might be, but there was one way in which Middlesex could prove their manhood; a challenge must be thrown down.

So, with almost the chivalry of a Field of Cloth of Gold, Yorkshire were invited to partake in a challenge match on neutral ground, at the Oval (just, it might be added, a comfortable stroll across the river from Middlesex's home at Lord's).

There was no reason why Yorkshire should accept. They had had a long season. They had played four matches more than Middlesex in the County Championship. They had also played MCC at Lord's, Oxford University, New Zealand, Scotland and MCC at Scarborough in the Festival.

But Yorkshiremen were not brought up to show the white flag.

Hugely delighted, Brian Sellers snatched up the gauntlet almost before it had left R. W. V. Robins's hand. Yorkshire batted first. They were 256 before the second wicket fell. Out of a total of 401, Hutton scored 121 and Arthur Mitchell 86.

Middlesex blenched before their masters. 185 in the first innings, 101 in the second was all they could muster, Verity taking 8 wickets for 43 runs. Mournfully, Middlesex licked their wounds. Never again was a challenge thrown out to Yorkshire.

Lord Sheffield's Australian team, 1891-2, photographed in the Botanical Gardens, Adelaide. W. G. Grace is seated centre.

SHIPMATES ASHORE

IN 1902 the MCC made their first official tour of Australia. Naturally Wilfred Rhodes was one of the first to be selected and he went again in 1907 and 1911, but his performances and outlook on these three tours were both remarkable and almost unrealistic.

In 1903 he was recognised as the best slow left arm bowler in the world. In the Test Match at Melbourne he took seven wickets for 56 runs in the first innings and 8 wickets for 68 in the second, besides having eight catches dropped off him. It was said that George Hirst was the only Englishman who did not drop a catch in that match, and, maliciously, that only because none went to him. Fifteen wickets in one Test Match was a record that stood for many years.

Wilfred batted at number eleven, helping R. E. Foster to add 130 in 60 minutes for the last wicket at Sydney. Wilfred was England's star, the man taken to bowl out Victor Trumper, Monty Noble, Clem Hill, Reggie Duff and Warwick Armstrong.

Both for Wilfred and the MCC the 1907-1908 tour was thoroughly unsatisfactory. Wilfred was more interested in his batting than his bowling, but had not yet mastered the art of making himself indispensable to England in that capacity, and his concentration on batting had inhibited his bowling skill. Neither in batting nor bowling was he worth his place in the team. Batting low in the order, he scored only 205 runs in the five matches, averaging 20, and his seven wickets in the whole series cost 60 runs each. England lost four of the five Test Matches.

In 1911, with Jack Hobbs, Wilfred was to form one of England's great opening batting partnerships. At Melbourne they put on 323 for the first wicket, Hobbs scoring 178, Wilfred 179. 'He is now as great a batsman as he once was a bowler. Australian cricketers themselves say a greater', said a contemporary report. He scored 463 runs in the Test Matches and, 1,164 altogether on the tour. In the five Test Matches he bowled only 18 overs, taking no wickets. Throughout the whole tour he took only four wickets at a cost of 80 runs each.

In 1920, at the instigation of the Australians, a tour was hurriedly organised. Age had wearied the stars of 1914, war had decimated the ranks of the promising youngsters. All five Test Matches were lost. Wilfred scored only 238 in his ten completed innings and his four wickets cost 60 runs each.

From then up to the Second World War, Herbert Sutcliffe, Maurice Leyland (christened Morris), Roy Kilner, Hedley Verity and Bill Bowes carried Yorkshire's banner to Australia. All performed with distinction, did all that could be expected of mortals, but for most of the time they were faced by that cricketing phenomenon, Bradman. Only when Jardine peppered him with bodyline, when Verity caught him on a sticky wicket or when he broke his foot trying to bowl, could England find a grain of comfort in the long spell of the Don's ascendancy. For nearly 20 years it was not so much England v Australia as England v Bradman.

Since the Second World War, both Len Hutton and Ray Illingworth have captained England and brought the Ashes back from Australia, and surely, had it not been for an aberration on the part of the Selection Committee, Geoff Boycott would have done the same.

But before the official tours, teams went to Australia either as a commercial

Jardine, who 'peppered the Don with bodyline'.

proposition, or on an unusual and exciting holiday for the Gentlemen amateurs – or both. Sometimes visits were made under the aegis of Melbourne Cricket Club, sometimes of Sydney Cricket Club and sometimes teams went purely as a business venture, the arrangements and sponsorship being in the hands of some money-conscious consortium.

Matches would be played where they would be most profitable, irrespective of the difficulties of getting there and the hardships involved.

At one gold-rush town, pebbles had to be swept off the pitch by the tourists before play could begin. At a primitive hotel, the proprietor apologised for the absence of baths in his establishment, 'Ah', laughed W. G. Grace, who was on his honeymoon and in an understandably affable frame of mind, 'don't worry. We Graces ain't no bloody water spaniels.'

It was an age when the bush came down almost to the coast, when Botany was regarded as a penal settlement rather than a fine merino wool, and when roads into the hinterland were practically non-existent.

The earlier teams bucketed and wallowed, pitched and tossed, sea-sick and miserable from one settlement to another in coastal steamers. Inland, when it was dry, the tracks would be deep in fine, white dust. When it rained, the mud would come up to the hocks of the horses and the axles of the wagonettes, and some of the players (probably the professionals) would have to dismount and put their shoulders to the wheels to get the rickety vehicles up the hills, while the Gentlemen fired randomly at the magpies and the parrots.

There were plagues of flies. There were dust storms. The visitors got drenched to the skin, or were lost in the bush at night, seeking their next port of call.

Three days were allowed for a match, but because of the rough, bumpy pitches, the game would often finish in less than two. Still, the prospectors and the rangers had to be entertained on the third day. So a pick-up match would be arranged where 12 or 15 of the locals would play six of the tourists (usually the professionals) at single wicket cricket, while the Gentlemen of the party went off shooting quail and emu, amusing themselves with boomerangs or trying to catch kangaroos by the tail.

Not always did the professionals take kindly to this. In one match, when the Gentlemen had departed to their sport, they dismissed their opponents for 29, then allowed themselves, to the annoyance of the natives, to be bowled out for a grand total of 2; and presumably went to their ale.

They fell down companionways on the ships, were thrown off horses in the bush, risked life and limb on fearsome pitches or when wagonettes overturned and deposited them on the roadside.

But they rarely took more than twelve men. The halt, the lame, the sick, the weary, the walking wounded always had to play. There was no room on these tours for the grumblers, the timid or the hypochondriacs.

The first tour to Australia took place in 1862, Roger Iddison and Edwin Stephenson being the Yorkshiremen among the all-professional twelve. Iddison was from Bedale. He was an efficient batsman and a cunning lob bowler. When playing he wore a light coloured Derby hat, a violently striped shirt and a spotted tie.

W. G. Grace – 'no bloody water spaniel'.

*R. Iddison (**left**) and G. Anderson.*

For a time he was captain of Yorkshire but later he became something of a rebel, being a leader in the strike of the Yorkshire professionals in 1865. In 1874 he was appointed secretary of the Yorkshire United County Club set up, under the patronage of Lord Londesborough, in opposition to the established county club. It survived for three years.

Stephenson was regarded as the second best wicket-keeper in England, besides being a useful bat.

The arrival of the team in Australia was under the auspices of a firm of refreshment caterers, who made a fortune out of their venture. Wherever the team went there were brass bands to meet them, public holidays were declared, balloons were released, flags flew, balls and banquets followed, and, whenever they attended a theatre they had to mount the stage. Iddison wrote home, 'We are made a great fuss of. The Queen herself could not have been better treated.'

On their return home the Surrey club, which had provided seven of the players, gave them a banquet at the London Bridge Hotel and a benefit at a famous opera house.

Matches were all against odds, and Iddison was the most successful bowler with 103 wickets. In the match against Victoria he took 22. Altogether Iddison scored 314 runs and Stephenson 203, besides being the wicket-keeper.

Two years later a second team went under the captaincy of Old George Parr of Nottingham. Parr, like many an old Yorkshire cricketer, knew the value of brass and had refused to go on the first tour because he had a higher opinion of his monetary value than had the sponsors.

George Anderson, also from Bedale, a pal of Iddison, was the only Yorkshireman invited. Like Iddison he was a rebel and in 1865 he had refused the Yorkshire captaincy. There had been some controversy about no-balling and Anderson said he 'would not play against those who have combined to sweep us from the cricket field.'

A report in 1862 said of a match at the Oval, 'the fine, cool steady and effective defence of Anderson was the very perfection of cricket and worth travelling miles to see', and, writing of him in 1904, a critic said, 'He was perhaps the hardest hitter who ever played for Yorkshire.' In those days there were no boundaries and once at the Oval he hit an eight, which would have been a nine if his partner had not run out of puff.

With his handsome beard, Anderson looked like a Spanish grandee. Much was expected of him in Australia and he was greeted with

Next Anderson, of Yorkshire the pride,
  Whose bat's a mighty help to any side;
His county of him always has been proud,
  And greets his play with acclamation loud.
No doubt the bowlers, to their cost, will find
  To drive the ball he's 'mazingly inclined.

Alas, the rough sea voyage and the interminable cross-country rides upset him. He was rarely well or fit to play cricket. But cricketers were not taken to Australia in those days to be nursed or cosseted. When Anderson was not fit to play, Old George Parr made him umpire.

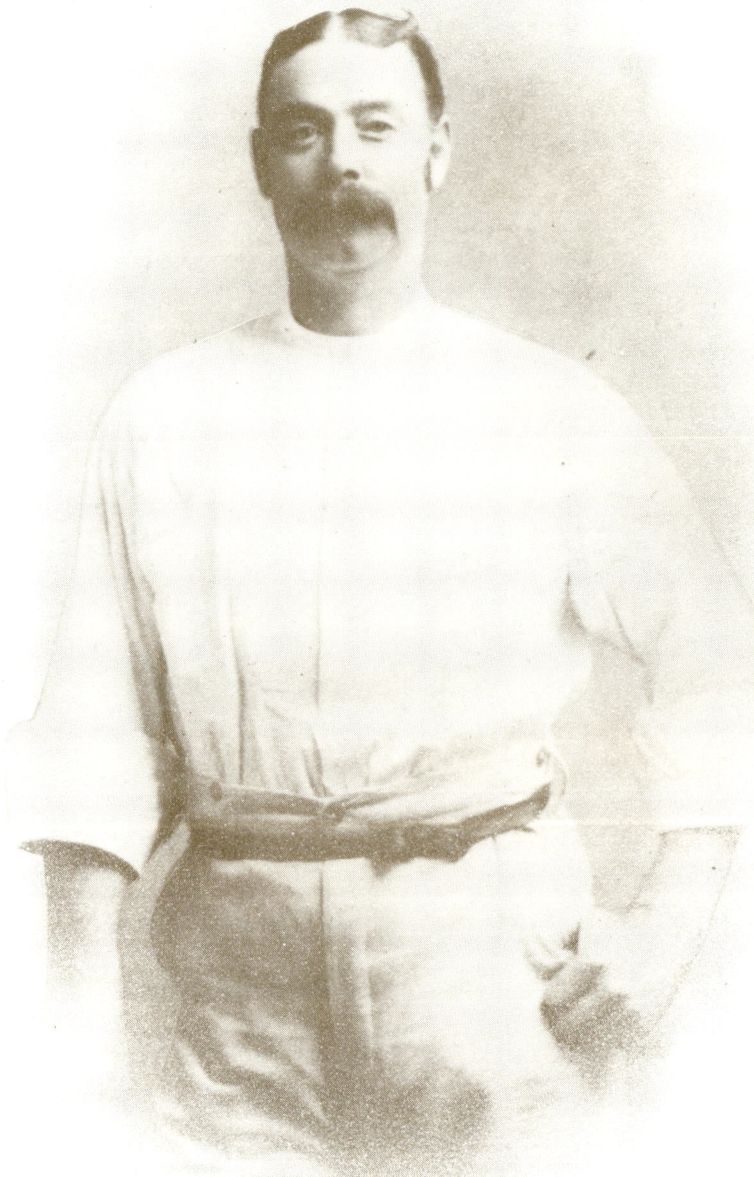

'TEN ALE CANS'

It was 1873 before the next team, captained by W.G., went down-under. From then onwards they followed almost at yearly intervals. Yorkshiremen were to the fore in these gay adventures. George Ulyett went five times, Billy Bates five, Bobby Peel four and Tom Emmett three.

Emmett, Ulyett and Peel were ideally suited to this jolly, nomadic life. Members of Lord Hawke's 'Ten ale cans', they would have been equally welcome in J. B. Priestley's *Good Companions* or on the boards at Leeds Grand Theatre or Bradford Alhambra.

Equable in temperament, cheerful in demeanour, carefree in outlook, they took life as it came and drank their ale where they found it. Of enemies they had none.

From 1878 to 1882 Tom Emmett had captained Yorkshire. Senior professional, renowned England cricketer, he had been one of the greatest bowlers in the country since 1866. In 1883, without rancour or resentment, he handed over the captaincy to the fledgeling Martin Hawke, and, for the next six years, trained him in tactics and guile, steering him past the pitfalls that a youth from Eton and Cambridge might stumble into in dealing with the rough, uncouth men he was to lead for the next 28 years. In time they gave him their trust, and he, in return, gave them his heart and his life.

Tom, accepting uncomplainingly his position and standing in that age of social inequality, was neither pedagogic nor sycophantic towards his young, untrained

(**Opposite**) *George (Happy Jack) Ulyett and* (**below left**) *Tom Emmett, two of Lord Hawke's 'Ten ale cans'.* **Below right** *Billy Bates, another of Hawke's gay adventurers.*

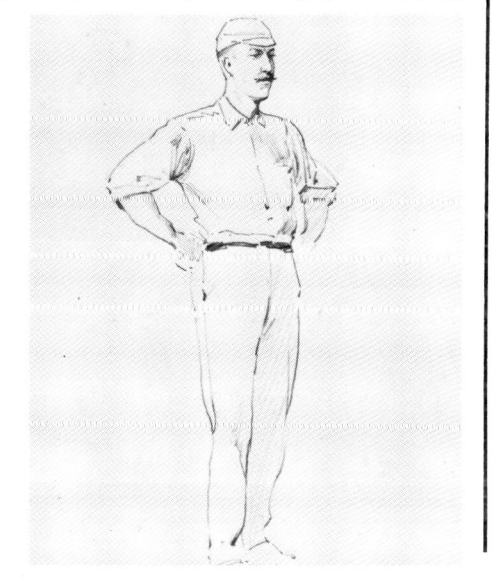

master. He taught by example, distilled wisdom from his long experience and set this scion of nobility on the path of sagacity and prudence on the field, power and honour in the administrative seats of the mighty.

When the black dog of remorse sat on the youthful shoulders of his new leader, Tom would lighten his burden with a merry quip; he would pull the leg of W.G. Grace when that martinet frowned his Jovian frown; he could, with his quaint humour, defuse an explosive situation.

He was of rubicund countenance, but had the natural dignity that comes from character rather than breeding. His friends were legion, yet he was never at their beck and call. One day a flatterer sidled up to him and asked to buy him a drink. 'Who tells thee I drink?' demanded Tom. 'Thy nose', sniggered the fool with the money. 'Aye, well, then', snapped Tom, 'my nose is a liar', and stormed away.

For over 20 years he was feared by every batsman in England. He departed, in his 48th year to Rugby School, to leaven the dead languages of Latin and Greek with the dying one of Yorkshire dialect.

For 20 years, from 1873, George Ulyett was Yorkshire's leading batsman. He played more innings for Yorkshire than Len Hutton, Maurice Leyland, Percy Holmes or Ray Illingworth.

He played in 25 Test Matches, scored 100 against Australia, and, in 1887 batted through the innings against Derbyshire to make 199 not out.

Had he been Irish he would have been called a 'broth of a boy'. Tall, florid and powerful, upright as a Guards RSM on parade, he was as lovable and cuddlesome as a baby elephant.

He batted in a manner that the Lord who had given him his formidable frame would have approved. Little men, average men, might be compelled to scrape and potter for their runs. God gave man (some men) an arm of iron. George had been given one and he used it as a giant in a fairy tale might wield his cudgel.

Cricket, to George, was a simple game. He was given a bat with which to hit a ball. All the theories, hypotheses and science which lesser men venerated, George eschewed. Often his county or Test Match captain would advise him of the intricacies and skills of the bowler he was facing, would counsel care, discourage aggression and speak earnestly of the enormous responsibility, the honour of England, that lay on George's shoulders.

Merrily George would knock the next ball out of the ground, and, as his captain fulminated would explain without a breath of apology, 'My Lord, I feel like hitting them.'

'If he had taken his cricket a little more seriously', said Lord Hawke, 'he might have been yet more valuable. To him, every match was simply a jolly game, and he did not care if he made a duck or a century.'

Known everywhere as 'Happy Jack', he began as a very fast bowler. In 1884 he had a hat-trick against Lancashire and seven wickets for 36 runs against Australia, but soon concentrated on his batting, averring (George Hirst had not been heard of at the time) that no one could bowl fast and then be expected to score runs.

He loved, when playing at Cambridge, to wander round the town in gown and mortar board, and breakfast with the undergraduates in their rooms. In those days dietetics was not another of these scientific fads with which medical men, nowadays, love to frighten us. One day when he was eating a plate of chops for breakfast, he was handed a jar of Devonshire cream. He looked at it in surprise, hesitated, and then ate the lot.

On tour it was doubtful if his assets compensated for his liabilities. He would go to any lengths to amuse himself with his practical joking.

In Sydney Harbour, at a picnic given in honour of the team, he was one of a party being towed in a small boat behind a steamer. Suddenly, to amuse himself, he began to scuffle with one of the personages in the boat and deliberately fell overboard into waters where sharks were not unknown. On being rescued he accused the innocent, and no doubt wealthy, passenger of pushing him overboard and demanded compensation.

Another time, shown some boxing gloves, he pretended not to understand their use. Kindly, his host offered to instruct him, whereupon George gave him a good hiding.

But when serious trouble brewed, George stepped into the breach. In Sydney in 1879, in a match against New South Wales, Murdoch was given run out by a *Melbourne* umpire (surely an unwise appointment considering the rivalry between the two cities). The Australian captain objected to the decision and demanded that the umpire be changed, a suggestion which Lord Harris, a martinet for the proprieties, curtly refused.

Temporarily the game was abandoned, and when the Englishmen again took the field a gang of betting louts and larrikins ran on to the field to maul them.

Among the tourists were Lord Harris, and amateurs C. A. Absolon of Kent, V. F. Royle of Lancashire, A. P. Lucas of Surrey, A. J. Webbe of Middlesex and L. Hone of Ireland. Only George and his pal Tom Emmett were professionals, but George took charge of the situation. He may not have read much history but the spirit that was to conquer at Rorke's Drift and, later, at Omdurman welled in his British heart.

Seizing the wickets he formed his troops in a tiny square, armed them with these weapons, took his stance at the front and challenged the hooligans to advance. Abjectly they slunk away and later, the match was resumed.

But the unsporting behaviour of the Sydney team rankled in George's honest soul. When the next Australian team came over he refused to play against them.

Poor George did not long outlive his career. A sudden chill turned to pneumonia and he died in 1898, before his 47th birthday.

Bobby Peel was the greatest understudy of all time. A slow left arm bowler with ability enough to play for England, he could not find a place in Yorkshire's team. Ted Peate, his senior by less than a year, was Yorkshire and England's left-arm bowler, and many have said that Ted, in his particular sphere, was greatest of all.

Bobby had played intermittently from 1882. Of his debut, Lord Hawke said, 'Even Wilfred Rhodes did not make a more promising first appearance than this lad, subsequently to be so famous.' But it was not till Ted's sudden oblivion that Bobby came to the forefront. In 1887 he had 85 wickets and in 1888, 171 – being one of only two bowlers in England to take more than 100.

From then until 1897, year in, year out, he was one of the leading bowlers in England's averages, besides scoring over 11,000 runs for Yorkshire and making

210 not out in the mighty score of 887 against Warwickshire in 1896. Against Nottinghamshire at Sheffield in 1888 he took 8 wickets for 12 runs in the first innings and 6 for 21 in the second, and in the Test Series of 1886 against Australia at Lord's, the Oval and Old Trafford he took 24 wickets for 181 runs.

In Australia he was happy as the day is long. The peripatetic, nomadic life was his ideal. He played hard, but with a comic élan and vivacity that endeared him to the crowds.

In one up-country match against Moss Vale he took 18 wickets for 7 runs. In another, when he ran a man out with a direct throw and asked, 'How's that?' the local umpire replied, 'A damned smart bit of fielding'.

In 1895, when he made the match-winning run against Turner, 'the Terror', in a Test Match, he rubbed salt into the wound by walking across the pitch and presenting Turner with his bat.

But in two consecutive Test Matches in Australia he made four ducks.

Bobby's departure from the Yorkshire team was sad and sudden. One morning at Sheffield he had not recovered from his libations of the previous evening, and George Hirst, in his kindly way, put Bobby back to bed and reported to Lord Hawke that he was 'poorly'.

The team had taken the field with the twelfth man as substitute, when Bobby, in his cricket flannels, staggered on to the field, announcing that he was perfectly fit to play. Stories of what happened next vary. One is that he took the ball and, instead of bowling at the wicket, bowled it at the sight screen. But one thing was certain, Bobby never played for Yorkshire again. He was not the first whose popularity with the spectators and hangers-on had brought about his downfall.

This, for Lord Hawke, was probably the saddest moment of his 28-year captaincy. Bobby was his protégé, and in spite of alcoholic aberrations, probably his favourite. When the players presented His Lordship with a gold cigarette case embossed with Yorkshire's arms as a mark of their regard, it was Bobby who made the presentation.

Each in his own way held the other in high esteem. It was a misdemeanour that Lord Hawke, who did so much to change the image of professional cricketers from that of illiterate, often drunken, louts to valuable and responsible members of society, could not overlook.

Nevertheless, though there was mutual sorrow, there was no rancour in the dismissal. Lord Hawke was instrumental in obtaining for Bobby an important coaching engagement, and they remained friends to the end.

SWANSONGS

Most Yorkshire cricketers, like old soldiers, simply fade away. Sadly, before putting themselves out to grass, they have continued playing a year or two longer than was wise. Time, as the hymn warns, 'bears all its sons away', but, before that, with evil malice, it has weakened sinews and softened muscles. As in the case of royalty, there is little interest in cricketers between the ages of forty and eighty.

They take their benefits, play for a few years longer, and are gradually usurped by youngsters whose bounding energy outweighs and replaces the veterans' fading craft and guile.

Probably the first of all benefits was arranged in 1865 for the five rebels who went on strike. A 'complimentary' match was organised for them at Hyde Park, Sheffield, when All England played Eighteen Gentlemen of the North, and, before official benefit matches were instituted, there were matches for Roger Iddison, Joe Rowbotham, Luke Greenwood, Eph (Mary Ann) Lockwood and Tom Emmett - almost always at Sheffield against Gloucestershire because of the attraction of W. G. Grace.

George Freeman. W. G. called him 'the greatest fast bowler I've met'.

Wilfred Rhodes 'took on his ageing shoulders the task of rebuilding Yorkshire'.

The first official benefits were for Louis Hall, that upright chapel-goer, which ran to £570 in 1891, and Bobby Peel, the popular prodigal who received £2,000 in 1894.

Often a final appearance was at a Scarborough Festival Match, when due but muted respect was sadly, sincerely, but nonetheless thankfully paid to a long, trustworthy and illustrious career.

But some were cut off in their prime. They never lived to receive the final accolades nor the eulogies their skill and effort had deserved. Unlike the rest of us, they did not grow old.

Roy Kilner first played for Yorkshire in 1911, before his twenty-first birthday. He was a swashbuckling left-hand batsman, a match winner with his antagonistic approach, his defiant attack, his desire and willingness to hammer to oblivion the bowling of Johnny Douglas, Dean of Lancashire, Frank Woolley, Sydney Barnes, Jack Hearne, Frank Foster and other masters.

In 1913 he scored 104 against Leicestershire, in 1914 169 against Gloucestershire, and was scoring over 1,000 runs a season.

He was Yorkshire's bright new middle order batsman, a cornerstone in a magnificent team with George Hirst, Wilfred Rhodes, Schofie Haigh, the up-and-coming Percy Holmes and those two magnificent young all-rounders, Major Booth and Alonzo Drake.

But four years of war decimated what could have been Yorkshire's greatest team. Schofie Haigh had gone by 1918, Hirst was on his last lap, Major Booth had died in battle, and illness had closed the wonderfully promising career of Alonzo Drake.

Yorkshire needed to rebuild. Wilfred only of the old brigade was left, and he was over forty. On his ageing shoulders Wilfred Rhodes took the task of rebuilding and refurbishing the Yorkshire side. His eye fell on Roy Kilner. Here was a great batsman, but, deliberately, Wilfred conjured out of him a great slow left arm bowler. He had not the spin of Wilfred, he had not his flair. His skill was instilled not intuitive but he became the greatest flight bowler of his generation. As a coach at Harrow School, Wilfred was regarded as something of a failure, but no one ever made so fine a brick with so little straw as Rhodes did out of Kilner.

Four times Kilner was to perform the double of 1,000 runs and 100 wickets in a season. He was to score 206 not out against Derbyshire in 1920, to take six wickets for 13 against Hampshire in 1922, 6 for 14 against Middlesex in 1923 and 8 for 40 against Middlesex in 1926.

In Australia in 1925, in the Third Test, he bowled England to within 11 runs of victory when they had been 124 behind on the first innings. In the Fourth Test, when England won by an innings, he scored 74 runs and took 5 wickets for 70.

With his red hair and jaunty cap his popularity was enormous. His benefit of over £4,000 in 1925 was not to be exceeded till the Hedley Verity Memorial Fund in 1945. Stories of his affability, his humour and Yorkshire fun were legion. A pottery firm made drinking mugs and cream jugs with his portrait on them.

Roy Kilner. 'His popularity was enormous.'

Major Booth, killed in action (as Lieutenant Booth, in 1916). He had established himself as one of England's leading all-rounders.

Alas, 1927 was to be Roy's last season. On a winter coaching engagement in India he contracted enteric fever. He came home to die in Barnsley Fever Hospital on April 6, 1928. 'All Yorkshire went to his funeral, and Yorkshire mourned deeply', said Sir Pelham Warner.

His last match for Yorkshire was against the MCC at the Scarborough Festival on August 31 and September 1 and 2, 1927. In a dreary, low scoring match Yorkshire were left to score 135 runs to win in an hour and three quarters. After Herbert Sutcliffe and Maurice Leyland had been quickly dismissed, Percy Holmes and Roy rattled off the runs in 70 minutes, Kilner finishing with 51 not out. It was a cheerful farewell in the swashbuckling manner that had marked his early pre-war cricket before bowling had come to demand too much of his attention; before strategy and cunning had usurped youthful joy and abandon.

In 1908, at the age of 21, Major Booth made his first appearance for Yorkshire. Major was a Christian name, not a rank. It was a foible of the time to give such military names. There were Captains and Sergeants, and one West Riding labourer, having the surname of Wharton, had the Christian name Lord conferred on him, no doubt in admiration of Philip, Lord Wharton who, by his will distributed Bibles to all and sundry provided they could recite a series of Psalms.

By the end of the 1914 season Major Booth had established himself as one of England's leading all-rounders. He and Alonzo Drake (the only Yorkshireman ever to take four wickets in four consecutive balls) seemed destined, as all-rounders, to lead another Yorkshire era of supremacy. In 1913 Booth had 1,228 runs and 181 wickets for Yorkshire, Drake had 1,056 runs and 116 wickets.

In 1911 Booth scored 210 against Worcestershire and, in 1913, 107 not out against Middlesex. Twice he did the hat trick. In 1912 he took 8 wickets for 47 against Middlesex and, in 1914, 7 for 21 against MCC.

In the winter of 1913-1914 he toured South Africa with the MCC team, which included Jack Hobbs, Frank Woolley, Wilfred Rhodes and Sydney Barnes, for whom Major was to be understudy. Barnes's international career was drawing to a close. Pencilled in as his replacement was Major Booth.

He played in the First and Fifth Test Matches, taking 7 wickets and scoring 46 runs.

His last game in Yorkshire was at Bradford against Sussex in the middle of August. Yorkshire batted first and Booth opened the innings with Benny Wilson, but while Wilson scored 208 (and Wilfred Rhodes 113) in a total of 443, Booth made only 3. It was a strange innings. In the huge total of 443, seven Yorkshire players scored 5 or less.

Sussex offered little resistance. Booth took 9 wickets in the match and Yorkshire won by an innings and 183 runs.

His last match of all was the return fixture at Brighton. Again it was a high-scoring match but Booth had little to be pleased about. Again, opening the innings, he made only 1 in a total of 461, and when Sussex responded, also with over 400, he took two wickets.

It was his last match. The Scarborough Festival was abandoned. A career of high promise had been cut off when its zenith should have been ten years in the future.

Towards the end of the 1914 season came the First Great War and in 1916 Booth was killed in action.

It is a macabre fact that although we glory in Yorkshire's succession of world-famous slow left arm bowlers, over the last 100 years only Wilfred Rhodes has played out his cricketing career with the county. Ted Peate and Bobby Peel were dismissed by Lord Hawke, Roy Kilner died of fever, Hedley Verity was killed in battle, Johnny Wardle's contract was not renewed after 1958 and Don Wilson betook himself to be head coach at Lord's.

When snow lies deep on the ground and even the mention of cricket brings home a little warmth to shivering, ageing bones, it is pleasant, if futile, to discuss who was the greatest of Yorkshire's slow bowlers – Peate, Rhodes or Verity?

Like all good philosophic discussion it has neither answer nor conclusion. They played under different conditions of pitch, batting technique and field setting. Whatever opponents and difficulties they faced, each, in his individualistic way, overcame them. None brooked a master; none wilted under attack. Content in their own invincibility, all three wrote their names large on the screen of cricket history.

It is noteworthy that in the 60 years from 1880, Yorkshire's slow left arm bowling was in the hands of just four bowlers – Peate, Peel, Rhodes and Verity (for while Kilner was a master bowler in his own right, his period of ascendancy ran concurrently with that of Wilfred Rhodes).

It is also a matter for speculation how many great bowlers these four master craftsmen kept in the shadows, for in that period every league club in Yorkshire had a left arm bowler capable of playing in the highest class of cricket, had the door

Hedley Verity, on whom descended Wilfred Rhodes's mantle, chatting with George Hirst at Scarborough.

to advancement not been kept firmly locked by the intrepid four. It was Neville Cardus who said that every time he peered into a pram in Heckmondwike, he feared that he was gazing into the cot of another world-beating slow bowler.

At the start of the 1930 season Wilfred Rhodes was 52. In both 1928 and 1929 he had taken 100 wickets in the season, but now the time had come to depart. Like Elijah by Jordan, Wilfred was to hand over his mantle. And Hedley Verity was as deserving a recipient as Elisha.

Verity was in his 26th year. He had served his apprenticeship in Lancashire League cricket. In his first season with Yorkshire, 1930, he was top of the All England bowling averages with 64 wickets at 12.42 runs each. In his next season he was playing for England. In the winter of 1932 he was in Australia with Jardine's team, keeping Bradman at bay while Larwood and Voce rested from their labours.

His greatest day was to come in 1934, at the Lord's Test Match. Catching Australia on a sticky wicket he took 7 wickets for 61 in the first innings and 8 for 43 in the second, equalling Rhodes's record at Melbourne 30 years before. It was England's first victory over Australia at Lord's since 1896.

In 1932 he took 10 wickets for 10 runs against Nottinghamshire, including the hat trick: in 1931 10 wickets for 36 against Warwickshire. Seven times he took nine wickets in an innings. And besides this genius and these prodigies he batted soberly and correctly, 'like Herbert Sutcliffe gone stale', said an unkind critic. But, in a crisis he opened the innings for England, and scored 100 against Jamaica on a West Indian tour.

He was 34 when war broke out; no more than at the middle period of a slow bowler's career, but he was of such an age that he could have sought sanctuary in a reserved occupation, or, as many sportsmen contrived to do, become a physical training instructor in the Forces. Instead he sought the heat of battle.

He was commissioned in the Green Howards, took part in the Desert Campaign in North Africa and in the landings in Sicily, and it was in this offensive that he was killed in July, 1943.

His last match for Yorkshire had been at Hove on August 30 and 31 and September 1, 1939.

In the first innings Sussex had scored 387 and Yorkshire responded with 392. It was an even game, moving gently to a draw. But rain came during the last night. While the wings of the Angel of Death were heard over the land, while Hitler fumed, Verity bowled 6 overs and took 7 wickets for 9 runs. Comfortably, the game was won by nine wickets.

While Armageddon shadowed the world, while the God of Wrath poised his mailed fist threateningly over humanity, while awe, insecurity, and a baffled aura of doubt of all things holy hung over the land, the Yorkshire team had to make their long, lonely way back home from the South Coast. Trains had been cancelled . . . transport commandeered . . . blackness enshrouded England.

They travelled through the night by hired coach, dropping off as near home as could be arranged. A final wave of the hand, and each team mate disappeared into the black, silent night. Surely it was the strangest and saddest farewell to the career of a genius who was also truly renowned for his sportsmanship, kindness and generosity.

EPILOGUE
'From the fury of the Northmen . . .'

Over 1,000 years ago the Northmen ravaged the soft under-belly of England south of the Trent and the Mersey. Halfdene, Guthrum and Rolf Gangar, fearsome in horned helmets, thundered southwards, laughter on their lips, blood on their swords.

From the Abbeys of Croyland, Winchester and Glastonbury, from the hill fortresses of Cissbury, Richborough and Portchester, the wail went up to Heaven –

From the Fury of the Northmen, good Lord deliver us.
   From fire and slaughter, from rape and ruin,
From roofless walls and gutted barns, good Lord deliver us.
   From homelessness and want, from sickness following want,
From death in ditch and mere,
   From the fury of the Northmen, good Lord deliver us.

But the northern invaders were bought off with danegeld. William, the usurper from Normandy came, thrust aside the token resistance of the southern knights, and issued his vindictive order for the wasting of the whole country north of the Humber: 'Every living man was to be destroyed, and every article that could help to support life. Homes were to be burnt and the implements of husbandry broken up.' In Domesday Book was the one word *Wasta*, and half a century later William of Malmesbury wrote, 'The ground remains bare to the present day'.

Recovery was slow, and when it came, the merchants of London Town turned the northlands into their workshop, waxing fat on the products of the pits, the mills and the foundries, rollicking in their fine nankeen while the miners, the weavers and the smiths toiled for the pittances doled out to them by the cunning knaves who prospered on the fruits of their toil and industry.

They boasted in their cricket of Nyren and Pilcher, of John Frederick Sackville, Duke of Dorset, of 'Silver Billy' Beldham.

They sang, in their vapid self-glorification,

And now the game's o'er, and victory rings,
   Each doubles her chorus, and Fame spreads her wings;
Let's now hail our champions, all steady and true,
Such as Homer ne'er sung of, nor Pindar e'er knew.

But although years were to pass, stern retribution was to come. George Hirst, Wilfred Rhodes, Schofie Haigh, Herbert Sutcliffe, Maurice Leyland, Roy Kilner, Brian Sellers, Bill Bowes, Hedley Verity were to descend on the mighty citadels of the south.

Again, in Yorkshire, we have gone into recession, but like King Arthur in Avalon, like Francis Drake in Plymouth Sound, we merely sleep.

Again we shall arise, surge southwards and, like Gideon, slaughter the Midianites and trample down the altars of Baal.

And again, but this time from Lord's, from the Oval, from the St. Lawrence ground in Canterbury, will rise the prayer,

From the Fury of the Northmen, good Lord deliver us.

Harry Sampson scored the largest innings ever played on the ice – 162 – for Sheffield Wednesday against Sheffield Town in February, 1841.

Also from The Whitethorn Press...

Laughter At The Wicket
by Harry East
Echoes from the Golden Age of Yorkshire Cricket.
£2.75. By post £3.00.

Queer Folk
by Maurice Colbeck.
A comicality of Yorkshire characters.
£1.85. By post £2.10.

Yorkshire Laughter
by Maurice Colbeck.
A further comicality from the Broad Acres.
£1.85. By post £2.10.

Queer Goings On
by Maurice Colbeck.
Yet another Yorkshire comicality.
£1.85. By post £2.10.

Steam-up in Lancashire
Railwayana from Lancashire Life.
£1.00. By post £1.25.

Just Sithabod
Dialect verse from Lancashire Life.
£1.50. By post £1.65.

Cheyp at t'Price
More dialect verse from Lancashire Life.
£1.50. By post £1.65.

Flower Arrangement — Free Style
by Edith Brack.
£2.20. By post £2.45.

The Mike Harding Collection
Folk songs of Lancashire.
£3.65. By post £4.15.

**Shakespeare's Avon
from Source to Severn**
by Richard Shurey
A guide for ramblers and country-lovers.
£3.00. By post £3.25

And, every month, the magazines:
**Yorkshire Life
Cheshire Life
Lancashire Life
Gloucestershire & Avon Life
Warwickshire & Worcestershire Life**

The Whitethorn Press Ltd., P.O. Box 327, Thomson House,
Withy Grove, Manchester M60 4BL.
And 33-35, Cross Green, Otley LS21 1HD.